Jewish Girls Who
Dreamed Big

And
Changed The World

Janice Baryshnik

Tellwell Talent
www.tellwell.ca

ISBN
978-0-2288-1402-3 (Hardcover)
978-0-2288-1401-6 (Paperback)

DEDICATION

Jewish Girls Who Dreamed Big and Changed the World is my passion project. It was conceived as a gift for my granddaughter Katie on the occasion her Bat Mitzvah. I soon realized that my four grandsons, Jacob, Benjamin, Joshua, and Saul, also had much to learn from these trailblazing and inspirational Jewish women. This book is dedicated to my five grandchildren and to all my present and future readers. I hope this book will help shape your aspirations and become as meaningful to you and your family as it is to me and mine.

TABLE OF CONTENTS

INTRODUCTION

In the past, with rare exception, girls were denied equal access to higher education and leadership opportunities. Nobel Prize winner Gertrude Elion had more than ten fellowship applications rejected because chemistry was considered a "male domain" and not an appropriate field of study for a woman. Evelyn Berezin, who developed the first stand-alone word processor, was restricted by the glass ceiling in the male-dominated tech industry of her day. Hedy Lamarr was expected to be a beautiful actress, not a brilliant inventor. If you were a Jewish girl, gender discrimination and restriction of opportunity were often magnified.

The biographical sketches in this book share a common theme. Each sketch is about a Jewish girl who set her mind on a goal and experienced tremendous obstacles along the path to its fulfilment. Whether in exile, in a laboratory, or in a library, each girl persevered, refused to compromise, defied expectation, exploded stereotypes, and was ultimately successful in achieving her objective. What's more, the world was changed because of each of these girl's dreams and triumphs.

Jewish Girls Who Dreamed Big and Changed the World was written with the hope that it would instil pride in the trailblazing, gender-defying achievements of Jewish girls of the past as well as inspire creativity and courage in the children of today and tomorrow.

RUTH HANDLER

RUTH MOSKO HANDLER

NOVEMBER 4, 1916 - APRIL 27, 2002

DID YOU KNOW THAT THE INSPIRATION FOR THE BARBIE DOLL CAME FROM A WOMAN WATCHING HER DAUGHTER AT PLAY WITH HER CUT-OUT DOLLS?

Ruth Mosko Handler was that woman.

And — you guessed it! Ruth's daughter's name was Barbara, nickname Barbie. I probably don't need to tell you that her son's name was Ken.

As a young girl Ruth had big ambitions for her future. She dreamed of becoming an entrepreneur, a female executive, and maybe even president of her own company. As a young mother, Ruth observed her daughter Barbie project her ambitions for the future onto her imaginary play with her dolls. The astute Ruth recognized that when her daughter and her friends played with dolls, they did not act out current childhood events. Instead, they role-played their hopes and aspirations for the future including college, career, and marriage. Ruth, the amateur child psychologist, intuitively understood that reflecting and experimenting into the future through pretend play was an important aspect of young girls' maturational process. Ruth, the business strategist, recognized a product void in the doll marketplace. That void was a doll that looked like an adult woman complete with breasts who dressed in a fashion forward manner. As you will soon learn, Barbie, the doll that filled this void, became a trendsetting cultural icon.

Let me backtrack a little and set the backdrop for both Barbie's entrance onto the world stage and Ruth Handler's fairytale success story. At first glance, Ruth seems an unlikely candidate to revolutionize the toy industry and start a Fortune 500 company. She was born into a poor family of European immigrants who came to America, travelling in steerage, to escape anti-Semitism and the pogroms in Poland. Ruth was the youngest of ten children in the Moskowicz (later Mosko) family so when her mother became ill, Ruth was sent to live with her oldest sister. Ruth did not complete college, left her sister's home in Denver Colorado, and went to California where she worked as a secretary. Certainly not the typical background conducive to nurturing a future successful businesswoman!

But Ruth was a born entrepreneur. She married her childhood sweetheart, Isadore Elliot Handler. The two were a dynamic duo. Elliot, as Ruth convinced him to call himself, was the creative force while Ruth was the marketing genius. When Elliot decided to build furniture for their home, Ruth shrewdly suggested he sell it commercially. When Elliot decided to manufacture picture frames with his partner Harold "Matt" Manson, Ruth convinced them to start a small company. The headquarters for this fledgling business was the Handler garage. Elliot used the scraps from the picture frames to make doll houses. Soon the partners realized that the doll houses were more lucrative than the picture frames. Deciding to focus on toy manufacturing, the two men formed Mattel, "Matt" from Harold Matson and "El" from Elliot Handler. Just so you are aware, in 1945, they did not even consider using a part of Ruth's name as the signature of the company. Even though her name was absent from the company, you can be sure Ruth was a driving force in the foundation and evolution of Mattel.

In 1947, Mattel had its first bestselling toy, the Uke-A-Doodle, a miniature ukulele. Madsen left the company shortly after and Ruth and Elliot created a hand-operated music box inserted into a toy. Yes, this toy is the Jack-in-the box, the toy that is a favourite of generations of children. Ruth and Elliot also capitalized on the western cowboy craze monopolizing shows of the day and created a toy gun called the burp gun. Ruth certainly had her finger on the pulse of popular culture!

Today there are many television shows specifically geared to children and teenagers. That was not the case in Ruth's time. So, when the Walt Disney company announced the *Mickey Mouse Club* series in 1955, Ruth recognized her golden opportunity. She knew that almost every child in North America would be tuned in to watch this show. Ruth gambled on her instincts and invested much of her family's resources to obtain sole sponsorship of the Mickey Mouse television series. That meant that every commercial on the Mickey Mouse program was an advertisement for a Mattel toy. That meant that during every commercial, kids would be watching other kids play with a Mattel toy they wanted for themselves and would then bug their parents to buy for them. This marketing approach was a game changer. It shifted the toy consumer from the parent to the child. Because the *Mickey Mouse Club* ran all year, it also created a year-round, rather than just a Christmas and Chanukah season, demand for toys. More specifically, it created a year-round demand for Mattel toys.

During this period, Ruth was still thinking about her idea for an adult doll. While on a family vacation in Switzerland in 1956, Ruth saw a doll in a gift shop which she recognized as the prototype concept she had imagined for her adult Barbie doll. She brought the sample home to be mass-produced as the very first adult-like doll in America. Barbie debuted at the American International Toy Fair in New York in March 1959. Marketed on the Mickey Mouse show, Barbie skyrocketed to success, as did her boyfriend Ken, who was introduced two years later.

Barbie has survived the test of time. It is for this reason that, in 1976, she was placed in the American government's time capsule as a meaningful representative of that period in history. Barbie was conceived of as a teenage fashion model but her popularity has lived on because she has kept pace with the prevailing culture of the day. During the John F. Kennedy presidency, she had a Jackie hairdo. In the Martin Luther King era, she had an Afro-American friend. When feminist criticisms surfaced in the 1960s and 1970s, her career choices changed to become more gender-neutral. For example, Barbie was an astronaut four years before Neil Armstrong ever walked on the moon. Barbie became a cultural icon, an ever-evolving reflection of North American society with professional careers, political endeavours, and clothes to mirror these shifts.

If Ruth were still alive, she would likely be bursting with pride to learn that Barbie has maintained this status. This past International Women's Day 2018, new dolls were introduced to help empower girls to close the "dream gap." These 2018 dolls are inspirational role models like Amelia Earhart, the first American pilot to cross the Atlantic; and Katherine Johnson, the Afro-American mathematician who helped to send the first man into space. Tessa Virtue, Canada's figure skating gold medalist, is also being honoured with a Barbie doll in her likeness because she too has shown that, with perseverance and hard work, girls can do or be anything they want. In honour of Barbie's sixtieth birthday in March 2019, Mattel announced it was launching updates of firefighter and pilot Barbies, careers which are apparently "still underrepresented by women today" (*InStyle*, March 2019). Ruth Handler's belief that through the doll "a girl can be anything" has expanded beyond even her wildest expectations.

As a personal point of interest, I had a chance to experience firsthand the everlasting appeal of Barbie this past August 2018. Barbie was the headliner for an exhibition in Helsinki, Finland when my husband and I were vacationing there. Our tour guide made it very clear to us that his ten-year-old daughter and her friends loved Barbie and the values she represented. Ruth's Barbie doll was, and still is, a metaphor for the changing role of women in society.

Ruth's story does not end with Barbie or with her resigning as President of Mattel. In 1970, she had a modified mastectomy for breast cancer. She could not find a suitable artificial breast replacement. Ruth being Ruth, she decided to form a company to develop and make her own prosthesis which she called the Nearly Me. Before Ruth, there was only one prosthetic for both the right and the left breast. Ruth recognized that even a shoemaker knows you have to make shoes for both a right and a left foot if you want to achieve a proper fit. The Nearly Me was so effective that Ruth personally fitted Betty Ford when she was first lady of the United States. Quite an accomplishment for a woman of Ruth's day to start two businesses in one lifetime!

Ruth Handler was a marketing genius who had a major influence in the development of modern branding and advertising. She tapped into the power of television and used this resource to reach her clientele, the children, directly. She was also responsible for galvanizing the movement for early detection of breast cancer and for heightening public awareness of the importance of a well-fitting breast prosthetic to a woman's self-esteem.

Self-esteem was also Ruth's goal in developing the Barbie doll. Ruth, and the new Barbie tagline, both assert that "when a girl plays with Barbie she imagines everything she can become" (*The Globe and Mail*, Toronto, March 3, 2019). Ruth Handler's enduring influence is simple. Her Barbie doll exposes girls to a wide spectrum of career options and allows young girls to dream big and practise taking risks.

HELENA RUBINSTEIN

HELENA RUBINSTEIN

DECEMBER 25, 1870 (OR 1872) · APRIL 1, 1975

DID YOU KNOW THAT A GIRL WITH LIMITED BACKGROUND IN CHEMISTRY AND NO FORMAL BUSINESS TRAINING COULD BUILD A WORLDWIDE COSMETICS EMPIRE?

Helena Rubinstein was that girl.

You probably have seen the musical *Fiddler on the Roof* and enjoyed its portrayal of Jewish life in the stetls (villages) of Eastern Europe. Do you remember Tevye, the father in the movie? He considered it his duty to arrange a marriage for Tzeitel, the eldest of his five daughters. Like many other shitachs (arranged marriages) of that period, Tevye's choice was based on practical and not romantic considerations. Sometimes in a shitach, the bride did not even get to meet her proposed husband until the day of the wedding. To complicate things even further, it was customary and almost mandatory that the eldest daughter in a family be the first of the sisters to marry. Fortunately for Tevye's other four daughters, Tzeitel had a different suitor, Motel the tailor, whom she loved and whom her father ultimately permitted her to marry. So, the lucky Tzeitel did not have to endure a loveless marriage to the much wealthier and much older butcher of her father's choosing.

This happy resolution was not the situation for Helena Rubinstein, born Chaya Rubinstein, in Krakow, Poland. The cultural expectation of "eldest daughter first to the chuppah" (marriage canopy) was problematic for Helena's parents. You see, the Rubinsteins had eight daughters and Helena was the oldest. At four feet ten inches, Helena was very small in stature but she was very large in willfulness and she refused to marry the man twice her age that her father had selected for her. Given what you have just read, try to imagine the implications on marriage prospects for the younger seven sisters created by Helena's refusal to marry the widower of her father's choosing.

To save her parents from ostracism and her sisters from spinsterhood, Helena went to live with relatives in Australia. She arrived at the small town of Coleraine, Australia with little English skills and even less money. What she did bring was her ambition, her porcelain skin, and twelve jars of the beauty cream she used to maintain her smooth complexion. This cream contained a secret ingredient: lanolin.

Helena quickly observed that because of constant exposure to sun, many Australian women had dry, flaky skin and were in need of a moisturizing cream. The women of Australia likewise coveted Helena's milky white complexion and wanted her moisturizing product so they too could achieve that appearance. A born entrepreneur, Helena recognized a need in the marketplace and a niche she could fill. With her mother's help, Helena began importing pots of the moisturizing cold cream from Poland.

Very soon, the ingenious Helena came up with a local source for her creams. Australia, as you may know, is home to many sheep, and sheep, which you probably don't know, secrete a wooly wax which is chemically the same as lanolin. Once she learned this and could acquire funding, Helena began to manufacture her own product under the name Cream Valaze. Valaze means "gift from heaven" in Hungarian. She even brought the chemist who developed the original product to Australia to develop a new and related range of products including soaps, cleansers, and moisturizers. And so, Helena Rubinstein's cosmetics brand was launched!

It is difficult to capture the creation and growth of Helena Rubinstein's cosmetics empire in a mere page or two, so the highlights of her vision and career will have to suffice.

Over her sixty years in the cosmetics business, "Madame," as she liked to refer to herself, changed the "face" of the cosmetics industry. In a time when society expected conformity, she encouraged women to embrace their individuality. She advocated that each woman should have her own make-up and hair cut to complement her own individual personality and style. She developed new and innovative products like waterproof mascara that helped women to lead a more active lifestyle. She was one of the first to warn against overexposure to the sun and developed one of the first sun tanning lotions. She lived and worked wherever business took her, including Australia; London, England; Paris, France; New York; and Connecticut. Several of her sisters were brought from Europe to help manage or establish her beauty salons worldwide. While living in London, England, Helena even took time from establishing her company to marry and later have two sons.

Helena Rubinstein was a gifted marketer, presenting herself as a "beauty scientist" who "diagnosed" different skin types and "prescribed" suitable treatments based on her findings. Products were developed to address oily, dry, and in-between skin types. Years before marketing became a course in business schools, Helena recognized the value of celebrity endorsements. Today we know that when LeBron James wears Nike or Rihanna wears Puma, the appeal and consequent sales of these items are greatly enhanced. In Helena Rubinstein's day, the concept of using a popular sports figure or a celebrity movie star to endorse a cosmetic, or any other product, was both novel and genius. Endorsements by actresses of the day gave Helena's potions and lotions greater legitimacy and appeal. The actress Nellie Stewart actually described Cream Valaze as being like "food" for the skin. Helena Rubinstein understood the power of building a brand long before the concept became cliché.

Helena Rubinstein was both a visionary and an eccentric. Her famous store on Fifth Avenue housed a restaurant and a gym. In her flagship salons, she introduced the exciting idea of "a day of beauty" which included exercise routines, diet plans, and a focus on tranquility, something like our present-day spa resorts. While these innovations may seem commonplace today, they were unique in Helena's time. Even though she collected and displayed art by Picasso, Matisse, and Miro in her salons, and even though she commissioned Salvador Dali to design a powder compact for her products, the no-nonsense Helena "brown-bagged" her lunch to work every day.

Helena was also philanthropic. Her charitable foundation funded a pavilion for contemporary art in Tel Aviv, Israel; underwrote programs for women and children; and sponsored the popular educational children's program *Sesame Street*.

Helena Rubinstein was a dynamic and sometimes difficult woman. When her bid for a Park Avenue apartment was rejected because she was Jewish, she overcame this "restriction" and retaliated by purchasing the entire building. At ninety-two years of age, when thieves broke into her apartment demanding her jewellery, she refused to hand it over, telling them they could kill her if they wanted but they could not rob her. She maintained a lifelong rivalry with fellow cosmetics giant Elizabeth Arden which has been immortalized in the Broadway play *War Paint*.

Helena Rubinstein was a female Chief Executive Officer (CEO) at a time in history when there were very few female CEOs. She intuitively understood female needs and desires and used this knowledge, together with her business acumen and charismatic personality, to single-handedly develop one of the great growth industries of the twentieth century — cosmetics. Helena Rubinstein grasped that lipsticks and lotions could enhance a woman's self-confidence and self-esteem and help her project her individuality. Today, we have come a long way in our understanding that a woman defines herself through her choices, whether in her appearance, her hobbies, her career, or her spouse.

RITA LEVI-MONTALCINI.

RITA LEVI-MONTALCINI

APRIL 22, 1909 - DECEMBER 30, 2012

DID YOU KNOW THAT THE DEATH OF HER NANNY FROM CANCER COULD
BE THE IMPETUS FOR A GIRL TO WIN A NOBEL PRIZE IN MEDICINE?

Rita Levi-Montalcini was that girl.

Rita Levi-Montalcini was the kind of girl who would not allow her life to be mapped out by anyone but herself. She was also the kind of girl who would not take "no" for an answer once she had set her mind on a course of action.

These qualities created a big problem for young Rita. You see, in the early 1900s, the expectations for girls' futures were very narrowly defined. Girls were expected to get married and have children. Rita's father, like many of his generation, also held to the old-fashioned belief that a university education and career would interfere with Rita's ability to be a good wife and mother.

But the ambitious and headstrong Rita imagined a different life for herself. When her nanny Giovanna, who she was devoted to, died of cancer, Rita was determined to become a physician and cure disease. Rita believed in herself and she wasn't about to let anyone or anything stand in her way. You could say she was a polite but pioneering feminist.

Still, the path to medical school was not easy for Rita. She had to plead with her father till he relented and agreed to allow her to attend university. Permission granted, Rita faced a further challenge. To qualify for entrance to the university, Rita had to master Latin, Greek, and mathematics. And — she had only eight months to do so!

During medical school, Rita became fascinated by the complexity of the brain and nervous system. So, when she graduated summa cum laude in 1936, she enrolled in a further three-year fellowship in neurology and psychiatry.

Then came the law that all Jews were terrified of. Mussolini, the dictator of Italy, decreed that Jewish people were forbidden from pursuing academic or professional careers. Just like that, Rita's fellowship was abruptly terminated because she was Jewish.

This was a formidable obstacle if there ever was one. But Rita was as resourceful and ingenious as she was passionate about medicine. So, when she was barred from the university, she assembled a makeshift laboratory in her bedroom. Here she studied the growth of nerve fibres in chicken embryos (chickens before they are hatched). Sewing needles were the tools she had access to, so sewing needles became her surgical instruments.

When the Nazis invaded Turin, Italy in 1943, Rita and her family escaped to Florence, Italy. Rita was often seen riding her bicycle from house to house pleading with farmers for eggs to feed her baby. Her "baby," as you probably guessed, was her research project. Fortunately, Rita continued her research and the family survived the Holocaust living underground and using false identities.

When the war ended, Rita was granted a research fellowship at Washington University in St. Louis, Missouri. Try to imagine a young woman who had just survived the terrors of the Holocaust crossing the ocean alone and coming to a foreign country more than seventy years ago. A daring and courageous undertaking by a daring and courageous young woman!

The fellowship was supposed to be for one year but Rita ended up remaining at Washington University for over thirty years. During this time, she and her biochemist colleague Dr. Stanley Cohen isolated and described the protein commonly known as Human Growth Factor. Human Growth Factor is the chemical tool our body uses to direct the growth of our cells and to build nerve networks.

This discovery was groundbreaking and revolutionary. It changed how scientists studied cell development and cell differentiation. It changed how scientists understood the mechanisms by which cell growth could go wrong and thereby cause a cancerous tumor or a degenerative disease like Alzheimer's. The discovery of Human Growth Factor also offered ways to potentially cure, or at least control, many diseases. All of this happened because of Rita's chicken embryos!

In 1958, Rita became a full professor at Washington University. This may not sound like anything special today, but this appointment was a rare accomplishment for a woman of Rita's generation. Rita also established a second laboratory in Rome. In Rome, Rita held many very distinguished scientific positions and was appointed a senator for life. She also founded and was president of the European Brain Institute. In fact, Rita was such a celebrity in Rome that Italians would joke that anyone could recognize the pope so long as Rita appeared beside him.

And if all this isn't enough, during retirement, when Rita could have spent her time reading novels or doing yoga while relaxing at the beach on the Amalfi Coast of Italy, she and her twin sister Paola, a famous Italian artist, started a program to mentor and provide grants to help teenage girls along their career trajectory. Rita and Paola wanted to ensure that girls could dream big and have the means by which to achieve their big dreams.

Rita Levi-Montalcini is a symbol of scientific achievement, feminist ideology, and social conscience. She was born into a patriarchal society with entrenched sexual biases and limited choices for women. Nonetheless, she was able to overcome societal barriers, parental opposition, and religious persecution to forge a career for which she and Dr. Cohen were awarded the Nobel Prize for Physiology and Medicine (1986).

Rita Levi-Montalcini was not afraid of nor deterred by adversity or difficult times. Instead, she let these obstacles and barriers bring out the best of her. She is proof that despite challenges, a girl can do or be anything she is capable of, if she sets her mind to it.

RABBI REGINA JONAS

RABBI REGINA JONAS

AUGUST 1, 1902 - DECEMBER 12, 1944

DID YOU KNOW THAT THE IDENTITY OF THE VERY FIRST FEMALE RABBI
WAS NOT DISCOVERED UNTIL ALMOST FIFTY YEARS AFTER HER DEATH?

Rabbi Regina Jonas was that woman.

In Berlin, Germany during the early 1900s, there lived a girl who wanted to learn everything there
was to know about Judaism. She loved to study the Hebrew language, Jewish history, and the Torah.
Her passion for Jewish studies was so strong that she set a goal for herself of becoming a rabbi.
When Regina was growing up, the highest rank of clergy, whether it was rabbi, priest, or minister,
was reserved for males. In this restrictive climate, Regina's goal seemed like an impossible dream. So
how did she become ordained as a rabbi and how was this discovered?

In 1991, Dr. Katerina von Kellenbach, a philosophy and religious studies professor from St. Mary's
College in Maryland, USA, was interested in studying the attitudes of both the Protestant and Jewish
religious establishments towards women seeking ordination in 1930's Germany. While researching
for her project, she found something totally unexpected and very exciting. In a remote section of
the Jewish Archives in East Berlin, the professor discovered an envelope. This envelope was a major
historical dossier! It contained documents related to Regina Jonas, including her teaching certificate,

her seminary dissertation, and most importantly, her rabbinical ordination diploma, dated 1935. This was when the world learned that the first female rabbi was Rabbi Regina Jonas.

Sometimes negative events have unexpected positive consequences. For example, when Regina's father died, the destitute family was forced to move to a new neighbourhood. Destiny intervened for Regina. The new apartment was located near an orthodox synagogue. The atmosphere of the synagogue appealed to Regina and one of the rabbis, Dr. Max Weil, recognized something special in her. Under his mentorship, Regina mastered the Talmud and rabbinic literature. Upon matriculation, she was certified as a teacher and pursued the only option available to her at the time, a teacher in an all girls' Hebrew school in Berlin. But Regina did not forget her goal. While working at the girls' school, she continued to study at a prestigious institution which trained young men (and one female — her) for the rabbinate.

In 1933, Regina wrote a dissertation debating the question "Can women serve as rabbis?" She used halakhic (Jewish civil and religious law) sources to address this issue. Using these halakhic "way of life" guidelines, Regina was able to deduce gender equality for the rabbinate. For Regina, this was progressive and enlightened thinking. For the male rabbis of the day, this was difficult to appreciate and even more difficult to accept. So while the rabbis at the seminary praised her dissertation, they did not agree to ordain her. Instead they stubbornly adhered to their conventional bias that only men could serve as rabbis.

Regina's response to the rabbis was logical and feminist. She argued that women were especially suited to become rabbis because of their compassion, intuition, social adeptness, and ability to establish relationships with children. Her message to the male rabbis was that these are prerequisites for the rabbinate and qualities which make female rabbis a cultural necessity.

Regina did not acquiesce to the rabbis' prevailing conventional thinking nor did she abandon lobbying her position to be ordained. Finally, in 1935, Dr. Max Dienemann, the Executive Director of Liberal Rabbis, agreed she had earned ordination.

But this was not the end of Regina's struggle. While she was now officially an ordained rabbi, no synagogue in Berlin would offer her a permanent pulpit because she was a woman. So, Regina decided to focus on delivering lectures and sermons as well as pursuing her pastoral work which included visiting the sick and caring for the elderly, all important rabbinic duties.

In 1940, like other Jews in Germany under Nazi persecution, Regina was forced into factory labour. Then, in November, 1942, she and her mother were arrested and deported to Terezinstadt concentration camp. Regina continued her rabbinic duties at Terezinstadt. One of her most difficult jobs was to meet the trainload of Jews at the station and help the newly arrived Jewish passengers adjust to the shock, disorientation, and horrific losses they were experiencing.

Regina was a tremendous source of Jewish cohesiveness at Terezinstadt. In the archives of Terezinstadt there is a hand-written document in which Regina Jonas summarizes her legacy under the title "Lectures by the Only Female Rabbi, Regina Jonas." This document lists twenty- four topics for the lectures she delivered in a two-year period. These include lectures on Talmudic dilemmas, Jewish ethics, pastoral issues, and the history of Jewish women. In delivering these lectures, Rabbi Regina Jonas wanted to offer hope to the inmates of Terezinstadt. She wanted to encourage learning even in the most life-threatening of circumstances.

Regina and her mother were deported to Auschwitz where they were murdered in December 1944. Regina was only forty-two years old but she had accomplished much.

Regina Jonas is the story of one woman's attempt to maintain Jewish solidarity and strength during the Holocaust. Hers is also the story of a girl who broke gender barriers and prejudices to become the very first female rabbi. Rabbi Regina Jonas believed people were blessed with abilities and callings without regard to gender. She would agree this applies not only to the rabbinate but also to any other passion a girl may have.

EVELYN BEREZIN

EVELYN BEREZIN

APRIL 12, 1925 - DECEMBER 8, 2018

DID YOU KNOW THAT THE WOMAN WHO DESIGNED THE FIRST TRUE WORD PROCESSOR ALSO STARTED HER OWN COMPANY TO MANUFACTURE AND MARKET IT?

That woman was Evelyn Berezin.

Pretend you are on your laptop writing an essay for school. You realize you need to make a correction. Maybe you forgot quotation marks, or maybe you want to move a paragraph around, or maybe you stained the page with remnants of your lunch. You delete, you cut and paste, or you print a second copy. It's quick and it's easy. What's more, you take the whole process of revision for granted.

Now imagine your great-grandparents and maybe even your grandparents trying to write an essay in school at a time when the word processor had not yet been invented. They had to write every word of the essay by hand and then start over again if they wanted to add a new thought or if they made a mistake big enough it couldn't be erased. Even if your grandparent knew how to use a typewriter, he or she still had to retype the essay if he or she made errors and, as you know, everyone makes errors. Fifty or more years ago, writing an essay or creating any written document was a frustrating, inefficient, and time-consuming exercise whether you were a student, a secretary, or a surgeon.

Then, in the late 1960s, a technological explosion occurred that literally revolutionized the way people wrote and prepared documents. Evelyn Berezin invented the first stand-alone dedicated word processor which she called the Data Secretary. Her word processor, which was driven by electronic components and programmable logic, was one of the most significant technological achievements of her time. If you want to see the original Data Secretary, it is on display at the Computer History Museum in Mountain View, California.

Evelyn Berezin was one of the giants at the dawn of the computer age. Even before she developed the Data Secretary, while working at various companies throughout the 1950s, Evelyn was a pioneer in devising systems which changed how people worked and produced. Let me more formally introduce you to Evelyn Berezin and tell you how this all happened.

Evelyn was a physicist, a computer engineer, an entrepreneur, a venture capitalist, and, above all, a visionary inventor. Evelyn's parents were immigrants from Russia. Her mother was a seamstress and her father was a cutter in the fur business. Evelyn's interest in physics was sparked by reading her brother's *Astounding Stories* science fiction magazines. Her parents had never heard of the word "physics" and were unaware this was an area of study which was, for the most part, restricted to boys. So, they did not know to discourage Evelyn when she announced she had decided to pursue it. Just the same, the road to a physics degree was not linear or smooth. Initially, Evelyn enrolled in economics at Hunter College with the goal of becoming a bookkeeper, a gender-and culturally-appropriate job for a girl of her day. Just so you are aware, because of gender bias, there were no science courses at the all-female Hunter College in Evelyn's day. However, when World War II broke out and male students became scarce, Evelyn was able to study mathematics through a special program at Brooklyn Polytechnic Institute as well as physics and chemistry at New York University.

In the 1950s, Evelyn got various jobs designing logic for computer systems built for specific tasks. For example, she developed computer systems to calculate bullet shell trajectories for the United States Army, to handle subscriptions at *Fortune* magazine, to automate banking transactions, as well as to monitor the amount of money bet on each horse at a race track. But Evelyn is most renowned for pioneering technology which changed how people made airline reservations. Evelyn designed an airline passenger reservation system for United Airlines delivered in 1962, in which three independently linked processors served sixty cities in the United States with a one-minute response time. Apparently, there were no central system failures in her system for eleven years. Just try to fathom the impact of these groundbreaking developments on the 1960s world and then read the first few sentences of the next paragraph.

Despite these brilliant inventions, Evelyn realized that her career was being restricted by sexual discrimination and the glass ceiling for women in the tech industry. For example, at one point in the early 1960s, a New York Stock Exchange executive hired her to be a vice president in charge of managing the computer systems that handled their communications. However, the Board of Directors of the Stock Exchange rejected her appointment, claiming that the sometimes-profane language on the trading floor was not appropriate for a woman's ears. This was the culture that Evelyn and other women of her generation battled.

In this environment, Evelyn reasoned that to advance in her career, she would have to launch her own tech start-up company. She called her company Redactron. The name Redactron was coined by her chemical engineer husband, Dr. Israel Wilenitz. It was chosen because the word "redact" means edit in several languages and editing was the original purpose of Evelyn's invention, the Data Secretary word processor. Redactron was launched in December 1969 with nine staff. It shipped its first product in 1971, and by 1975 it had grown to include a workforce of five hundred people. Think about it. In the 1960s and 1970s being a woman in the male-dominated tech industry was challenging and unique, but launching your own company and developing and marketing your own product was trailblazing.

For several years, Evelyn was "the lioness of the young tech industry, featured in magazines and news articles as an adventurous do-it-yourself polymath with the logical mind of an engineer, the curiosity of an inventor, and the entrepreneurial skills of a CEO" (*New York Times*, December 10, 2018). In 1976, she was featured in *Bloomberg Businessweek* as among the top one hundred business women in the United States. But after she sold the company to Burroughs Corporation that same year and stayed on in her division, she experienced the same gender-related prejudices she had escaped earlier. She left Burroughs describing herself as the only female in a company of "old boys" who were unwilling to accept her wisdom and ideas.

Undaunted, she reinvented herself and from 1980 to 1987 was President of Greenhouse Management Company, a venture capital fund which invested in early stage tech companies. During her lifetime she also held nine computer-related patents, was on the Board of Directors of several public companies, and was inducted into the Long Island Technology Hall of Fame (2006), as well as the Women in Technology Hall of Fame (2011). She was also named a Fellow at the Computer History Museum (2015).

Evelyn Berezin gives new meaning to the expression "the mother of invention." As a female pioneer in the field of Science, Technology, Engineering, and Math (STEM), her contributions changed the world. Evelyn Berezin is the quintessential role model for the acronym STEM, which is the focus of educational practices targeted in schools today. Evelyn Berezin deserves much recognition as a force behind young women studying and pursuing careers in these disciplines.

JUDITH LEIBER

JUDITH MARIANNE LEIBER

JANUARY 11, 1921 - AUGUST 28, 2018

DID YOU KNOW THAT THE WOMAN WHO DESIGNED THE CUPCAKE-SHAPED PURSE WORN IN *SEX AND THE CITY* ALSO CREATED ANIMAL-SHAPED BAGS WORN BY FIRST LADIES OF THE UNITED STATES AT THEIR HUSBANDS' PRESIDENTIAL INAUGURATIONS?

Judith Leiber was that woman.

Imagine you are at a fancy cocktail party and one of the guests leaves her purse at her table while she goes off to socialize with others. To the guest's surprise, when she returns to her table, the purse is not where she left it. Instead, it is being circulated and admired by everyone in the room. That is because Judith Leiber, the doyenne of the purse industry, best known for her little "minaudieres," or small clutch purses, elevated the purse to the status of a work of art. Today you can see her works of "art" on display in the Metropolitan Museum of Art in New York, the Smithsonian Institute in Washington, and the Victoria and Albert Museum in London, England.

Judith was born Judith Marianne Peto in Budapest, Hungary. Because there were restrictions on Jewish students entering university in Budapest in 1938, her parents sent her to King's College in London, England to study chemistry. The objective was for her to go into the cosmetics industry.

But, with the rise of Hitler and the outbreak of war, after her first year of university, Judith chose to remain with her family and not to return to England.

Instead, Judith became an apprentice at a prestigious handbag company in Budapest called Pessl. Her career in the purse industry began with her sweeping the floors and making glue. Soon, her initiative and intelligence became apparent and she was given the opportunity to learn how to cut leather, make patterns, as well as frame and stitch a purse. In other words, she soon mastered the craft of purse making from start to finish. She became the first woman to become a master craftsperson in the Hungarian Handbag Guild. Her famous green "toolbox" of essentials for handbag construction was part of her graduation diploma.

During the terrors of Hitler, in 1944, the Peto family got a Swiss Schutzpass which put them under diplomatic protection for a short period of time. If you want to see this document, you can visit the Holocaust Museum in Washington, D.C. where it is on display. Then, like so many other Hungarian Jews, the Petos lived in a cramped and damp ghetto basement with sixty other people. To alleviate her misery and keep herself occupied during this time, Judith designed handbags in her head. She has been quoted as saying "Hitler put me in the handbag business" (*New York Times*, Enid Nemy, August 30, 2018).

The Peto family was liberated by the Soviet army. In 1945, Judith met Gershon Leiber who was a radio operator from the United States Army. He was also an aspiring artist. They married and moved to New York in 1947. Judith had only her wits and her green tool box to rely upon for making a living when she arrived in New York.

Initially, Judith worked in an accessory factory in New York but her creativity was stifled in this position. Her bosses wanted her to copy European designs while she wanted to create her own designs.

Eventually, Judith was hired by the famous American designer Nettie Rosenstein. She worked for Nettie rising through the ranks for more than a decade. Then came her special opportunity. In 1953, Judith designed a purse for Mamie Eisenhower for her husband's presidential inaugural ball. Once people discovered that it was Judith who had created the pink minaudiere covered with pearls and rhinestones for the inauguration, her popularity and prestige were established.

In 1963, with Gershon as the business force and herself as the creative element, Judith launched her own company. Over the years, she made purses for famous actresses as well as many presidents' wives. The tuxedo cat purse designed for Hillary Clinton was modelled after "Socks," the First Family's pet cat, while the "Millie" dog-shaped bag was modelled after Barbara Bush's springer spaniel dog Millie.

In 1993, Judith Leiber won the Lifetime Achievement Award from the Council of Fashion Designers of America. It was the first time that the award was given to a handbag designer. Then in 2005, Judith and Gershon established the Leiber Collection Museum in East Hampton, New York to showcase her craft and her vision. It was Judith's goal to have one example of every one of her more than three thousand five hundred designs on display in her museum.

Judith Leiber is the story of a resilient young woman who was able to master a "man's" trade and then transport her skills to her adopted country. Hers is the story of survival, vision, and determination to "make it work" — a powerful recipe for success regardless of a person's area of expertise.

ESTHER (EPPIE) LEDERER

ESTHER "EPPIE" LEDERER (ANN LANDERS)

JULY 4, 1918 - JUNE 22, 2002

DID YOU KNOW THAT A WOMAN WHO WON A CONTEST TO WRITE
AN ADVICE COLUMN IN 1955 WAS NAMED THE MOST INFLUENTIAL
WOMAN IN AMERICA BY THE WORLD ALMANAC IN 1978?

Esther "Eppie" Lederer, better known by the pen name Ann Landers, was that woman.

Who do you confide in when you are having a problem with your peers, your parents, or even your pimples? If you are fortunate, you can turn to a sibling, a best friend, or your mom and dad for support and direction. Unfortunately, some people do not have the luxury of this option. Others prefer to ask a more anonymous, less familiar individual for help and advice. For these reasons, many people turn to "agony aunts" to help them address their personal issues. An agony aunt is someone who writes a column in a newspaper or magazine through which she or he dispenses advice and sometimes consolation to readers who have requested help with their personal problems.

Eppie Lederer was an agony aunt who wrote the column Ask Ann Landers for forty-seven years beginning in 1955. At her peak, she had a loyal readership of some ninety million people and her column was syndicated in one thousand two hundred newspapers around the world. With that exposure, it is little wonder that the World Almanac survey had named her the most influential woman in America. It was as if the Ask Ann Landers column was "tweeting" personal perspectives and opinions on hot topics before the concept of Twitter ever existed.

All of this happened because Eppie was searching for a productive outlet for her boundless energy. As fortune would have it, the creator of the Ann Landers column in the *Chicago Sun-Times* passed away at just this period in Eppie's life. Eppie entered a *Chicago Sun-Times* contest to select a successor to assume the Ann Landers' identity. She was the twenty-ninth of twenty- nine candidates for the position. At the time of her application, Eppie was an affluent housewife and mother who had never had a paying job or written anything for publication. The other contestants were all employees of the paper. Like the other twenty-eight contestants, Eppie was given a stack of letters from readers seeking advice and told to respond to them. To do this, Eppie called upon her many prominent social contacts in Chicago including a judge to address a legal question, a clergyman to answer a religious query, and so on. She assured the editor of the newspaper that she knew these individuals personally and had permission to use their expertise. The editor was justifiably very impressed and Eppie was offered the job. She remained at *Sun-Times* until 1987 when she left to work for a rival newspaper, the *Chicago Tribune*.

Esther "Eppie" Friedman and her twin sister Pauline (who became the voice of the Dear Abby advice column) were born in Sioux City, Iowa to Russian immigrant parents. Eppie credited her parents and her middle American heritage for her high morals, her commonsense judgment, and for the plain speak, no nonsense advice she dispensed in her column.

Working from her lakeside Chicago apartment, and, as the story goes, frequently while relaxing in the bathtub in this apartment, Eppie looked for letters to include in her column that people could relate to and that taught a lesson. As late as 1993, she was receiving queries from two thousand readers a day. Apparently, Robert Kennedy jokingly suggested he turn to Eppie for counsel on whether to run for president of the United States in 1968.

The Ann Landers column addressed universally relevant domestic issues including child-rearing practices, difficult mothers-in-laws, annoying neighbours, overly demanding bosses, and unfaithful husbands. It also tackled controversial social issues of the day like racism, anti-Semitism, drug use, domestic violence, capital punishment, homosexuality, and women's rights and roles. Through her column, Eppie became an advocate for the causes she believed in, like gun control, funding for cancer research, and abortion rights. Eppie was not shy to express her opinion on these matters, and because she was so admired and her opinion was so respected, her column had a profound influence on the attitudes of the day. The Ask Ann Landers column reflected the shifting views and perspectives of both herself and society with regards to the controversial social, political, and moral issues of the day. The column became a snapshot and barometer for the changing values and mores of America. "Her column had a finger on the popular pulse" according to Cornell University professor David Grossvogel who computer- analyzed the "changing dialogue" in ten thousand of the Ann Landers columns. In the same newspaper, her editor, Rick Kogan similarly described the Ask Ann Landers column as "a telling and important body of work" and "one which a future anthropologist could study to learn about what life was like in America between 1950 to 1990" (*Chicago Tribune*, June 22, 2002).

Eppie believed that getting a person to articulate his or her problems on paper was the first step to coping with or solving them. The magazine *Psychology Today* once credited Eppie with having "more influence on the way people work out their problems than any other person of her era" (quoted in the *Seattle Times*, June 23, 2002). All the same, she was a strong believer in counselling. Through her column, she also made it socially acceptable and respectable for people to seek therapy when a problem proved too complex or challenging to address in a letter to Ann Landers in the newspaper.

In a commencement address, apparently Eppie once told the graduating students that they should expect trouble in their lives because trouble happens to everyone. Her message to the students was simple. She advised the students that it was not what happens to them that counted, but rather how they dealt with it that mattered. Wise counsel from a wise agony aunt.

In 2002, the Chicago City Council resolved to honour Eppie Lederer for epitomizing the best of Chicago with her bold opinions and wise counsel. A street sign named "Ann 'Eppie' Landers Way" was installed in front of the Chicago Tribune Tower, headquarters of her home paper since 1987. If you visit the Windy City you should stop at the corner of North Michigan Avenue and East Illinois Street to see the street sign.

SIMONE JACOB VEIL

SIMONE JACOB VEIL

JULY 13, 1927 - JUNE 30, 2017

DID YOU KNOW THAT A SIXTEEN-YEAR-OLD GIRL TATTOOED AS PRISONER 78651 AT AUSCHWITZ IN 1944 WOULD SURVIVE TO BECOME THE FIRST FEMALE PRESIDENT OF THE EUROPEAN PARLIAMENT IN 1979?

Simone Jacob Veil was that girl.

In North America many of us have never even heard of Simone Veil. But in France where Simone was born and where she lived after the Holocaust, she is revered as a political icon. She is so popular and so well-respected that there are two Euro coins and a postage stamp with her image in circulation. There is also a plaza in Paris named after her and even the name of a subway station was changed to "Europe-Simone Veil" to honour her memory and her contributions. Most importantly, there is a piece of landmark legislation, the "Veil Law," which bears her name.

Simone Veil was an unintentional feminist who was responsible for a groundbreaking series of "firsts" for women of her generation. She was the first female minister of health in France. In fact, she was the first female minister of any portfolio in France. She was the first woman to have a parliamentary bill named after her. She was the first woman elected president of the European Parliament, now the European Union (EU). She was the first president of the Shoah (Holocaust) Foundation in France. Though not the first, she is also one of only five women buried in the Pantheon, a mausoleum which houses France's most significant historical figures. In the Pantheon, Simone rests in the company of Nobel Prize winner Marie Curie. In short, Simone Veil is beloved because she was a champion of the rights of women, a defender of the weak, a crusader for stability in Europe, and the president of the French foundation for preserving the memory of the Shoah. And — let's not forget, she describes herself as first and foremost a devoted wife and mother of three sons. Moreover, Simone accomplished all this when politics in France (and elsewhere) was a "men's club" and characteristics like independence, assertiveness, and strength of conviction, while admired when demonstrated by men, were criticized and denigrated when exhibited by women.

Just how did Simone come to accomplish so much? Here is a short history. In the 1940s, the Vichy government in France was collaborating with the Nazis in Germany. Simone and the rest of the Jacob family were living under false identity papers. Simone's father, a prominent architect, was expelled from his profession by the government because of its anti-Semitic laws and regulations. Later, in 1943, Simone, her parents, brother, and one sister were arrested and sent to Auschwitz concentration camp. Another sister was arrested as a resistance fighter and sent to a different concentration camp. Her mother, father, and brother perished during the war; Simone and her sisters survived and were liberated. The horrific events of her life at Auschwitz had a profound effect on Simone. As you will soon read, the experiences of the Holocaust informed Simone's political beliefs and shaped her purpose in life.

After the war, Simone achieved a law degree and embarked on a career in which she was first a lawyer, then a magistrate, and then a politician. It was her mission in life to defend the weak and the needy. As a magistrate in the Ministry of Justice, Simone specialized in human rights. Her efforts were directed at improving the lives of prisoners, especially female prisoners, and defending disadvantaged children and people with physical or mental disabilities, all of whom were groups which had been targeted for extinction by the Nazis. When she became director of civil affairs, Simone drafted legislation which guaranteed the adoptive rights of women as well as the right of a woman to a controlling voice in legal matters regarding her kids. Over the course of her career, she also expanded health care, child care, and maternity benefits. While these privileges and rights may seem self-evident and ensconced in our way of life today, it is important to understand them as radically novel and feminist concepts when viewed from the perspective of the status quo of Simone's time in France.

By far Simone's most notable contribution to the civil liberties of women in France was her shepherding of the bill that legalized a woman's right to a safe and legal abortion. This was the battle that defined her generation. When Simone presented her argument for legalizing abortion in the government chambers, there were four hundred and eighty-one men but only nine women present. With those odds, just try to imagine the arguments, slandering, and name-calling that took place. Simone's car was even vandalized. Nonetheless, the bill passed into law in January 1975 and became known as the Veil Law. Today, the Veil Law is considered the cornerstone of all women's rights and emancipation in France, and Simone Veil is considered the architect of these rights.

The experience of the Holocaust also gave Simone a second purpose. Despite the atrocities thrust upon her family and her fellow Jews, Simone envisioned a world, and especially a Europe, shaped by tolerance, integration, and strength of remembrance (International Auschwitz Committee, 2017). She fought for stability and reconciliation, especially of France and Germany, during her term as president of the European Parliament.

Simone never forgot her roots and never had her Auschwitz tattoo removed. She became the voice of remembrance when she became the first President of the French Foundation for the Memory of the Shoah (2000-2007). The Shoah Foundation strives to promote education and conserve archival information about the Holocaust, to promote the actions of righteous Gentiles, to assist Holocaust survivors, and to combat anti-Semitism through cross-cultural dialogue. Funds from the foundation also helped to build the Holocaust memorials in Paris and Drancy, France. If you go to the Holocaust memorial in Paris you will see that each member of the Jacob family is listed on the Wall of Remembrance. You may also learn more about the remarkable story of the Presidente D'Honneur of the Shoah Foundation, Simone Veil.

One last thing you should know about Simone: she was the sixth woman to be inducted into the Academie Francaise, whose members are known as "the Immortals." The Immortals are the guardians of the French language and are represented by French cultural and intellectual icons. On her ceremonial sword, which is the symbol of the Immortals, Simone had engraved the three things which shaped her life — the motto of the French Republic (Liberty, Equality, Fraternity); the motto of the European Union (Unity in Diversity); and, of course, her tattoo number from Auschwitz. In a speech delivered during her induction into the Immortals, one writer described her "as a figure on the prow of a ship projecting history into the future" (Jean d'Ormesson, *The Atlantic*, July 2, 2018). This description succinctly captures the contributions of a woman who metaphorically wrote the history which changed the world in which she lived.

It is now our job to continue Simone's fight for a better world. It is up to us to advocate for human rights, not just for women, but for all victims of oppression. It is up to us to advocate for tolerance amongst people of all nations, for people of all nations, all colours, and all religions. That is what we today can learn from Simone Veil's legacy.

LEONIE (NELLY) SACHS

LEONIE (NELLY) SACHS

DECEMBER 10, 1891 - MAY 12, 1970

DID YOU KNOW THAT A GIRL WHO WROTE PUPPET SHOWS AS A CHILD IN BERLIN, GERMANY COULD GROW UP TO WIN THE NOBEL PRIZE FOR LITERATURE IN STOCKHOLM, SWEDEN?

Nelly Sachs was that girl.

The story of Nelly Sachs is both bitter and sweet. It is sweet because in 1966, Nelly, together with another Jewish author named Shmuel Agnon, jointly won the Nobel Prize for Literature. It is bitter because Nelly's body of work bore witness to the suffering of the Jewish people during the Holocaust.

Nelly was the only child of a German industrialist family. She was considered to be of a delicate constitution and for this reason was tutored privately at home in Berlin until she was twelve years old. Her first exposure to music and dance also came from her home, particularly from the influence of her father who used to play piano while Nelly danced to his rhythms. In fact, dance was such a passion that Nelly's first ambition was to become a dancer.

Nelly's love of literature also came from her home, especially from the treasures she discovered in her father's library. Her talent for writing was apparent from an early age when she began to write poetry as well as plays to be performed by puppets. As a young teenager, Nelly was inspired by the literary work of Nobel Prize winner Selma Lagerhof of Sweden. Nelly's first poetry was in the style of this mentor. In fact, Nelly initiated communication with Lagerhof as a fifteen-year-old and subsequently maintained a lifelong friendship with this Nobel laureate who immediately saw the potential in her young protégé. It is Nelly's relationship with Lagerhof which rescued her from the Nazis and saved her and her mother's lives.

At one point in the late 1930s after her father had died, Nelly was interrogated by the Nazi Gestapo and she and her mother had their apartment plundered by them. This was such a traumatic event for the emotionally vulnerable Nelly that she became mute and did not speak for five days. Nelly immortalized this loss of her voice in one of her great poems.

In May 1940, Nelly and her mother received deportation orders from the Nazis. Selma Lagerhof, with the help of the royal family of Sweden, intervened to save Nelly and her mother from deportation and certain death. With Lagerhof's and the King of Sweden's help, mother and daughter left for Stockholm, Sweden on one of the last departing flights. When they escaped Germany, the once aristocratic and wealthy Sachs women carried with them only a few German marks, a thermos of tea, a few clothes, and some family memorabilia.

In Sweden, Nelly supported herself and her mother by writing poetry but primarily by translating Swedish poetry into German. During this time, she became interested in, and influenced by, Hasidic stories and Kabbalistic mysticism, both of which are reflected in her poetry. But it was not until her mother died in 1950 that Nelly began to focus exclusively on her career as a poet and playwright. Her major theme was the Holocaust. Nelly wrote in a modern style of oppression, persecution, exile, and death. She became the voice for the sorrows of the Jewish people.

The vulnerable Nelly had her own demons, evident since childhood. She maintained her creativity even though she was institutionalized for mental health issues from 1960-1963. In her lifetime, Nelly received numerous awards. In 1966, she shared the Nobel Prize for Literature with Shmuel Agnon. Referring to her prize Nelly commented that, "Agnon represented Israel, whereas, I represent the tragedy of the Jewish people" (quoted in the *New York Times*, May 13, 1970). Nelly felt that her experiences with the Nazis transformed her into the voice for the grief and yearning of the Jewish people.

One of Nelly's great tragic works is entitled *Eli: A Mystery Play of the Suffering of Israel*. In this play, she instructs us that the future cannot be built on the ruins of hatred and revenge. So, although Nelly Sachs wrote of the atrocities committed by the Nazis, she also wrote of the beauty of humanity. Her work both mourns the losses of the past and offers hope for the future. In fact, in 1965, a year before she was awarded the Nobel Prize, Nelly received the Peace Prize of German Publishers. She addressed her acceptance speech to young Germans when she stated:

"Together, full of grief, let us remember the victims, and then let us walk into the future to seek again and again a new beginning — maybe far away but yet ever present. Let us find the good dream that wants to be realized in our hearts. (*New York Times*, May 13, 1970)".

You may also find it interesting that on December 10, 2018, Nelly Sachs was honoured with a Google Doodle on what would have been her 127th birthday.

Forgiveness and harmony were present both in Nelly Sachs' message in *Eli* and in her poetry. She held optimism for mankind despite the atrocities some of mankind had committed. If she were alive today, Nelly Sachs' message to you would be simple. She would agree that there may be times when you may feel that you, or someone you care about, is being bullied or marginalized. Try your best to understand the reason for the transgression, and try to work towards, and look forward to, a better future.

JEAN SLUTSKY NIDETCH

JEAN SLUTSKY NIDETCH

OCTOBER 12, 1923 - APRIL 29, 2015

DID YOU KNOW THAT THE FOUNDER OF WEIGHT WATCHERS HELD ITS VERY FIRST MEETING IN THE LIVING ROOM OF HER HOME AND THAT TODAY THERE ARE 36,000 MEETINGS A WEEK WORLDWIDE?

Jean Nidetch was that woman.

When you were a little child, how did your mother comfort you when you were upset or sad? According to Jean Nidetch, her mother used food and treats as a source of solace. So, when Jean cried because she received a poor grade on a test, was excluded from a birthday party, or did not get chosen for a school team, her mother would offer her cookies or ice cream to help soothe her hurt feelings. Apparently, Jean was so overweight in elementary school that she would not go on a merry-go-round because she had difficulty mounting the horse and was afraid people would laugh at her. In high school, she struggled to get out of her desk during unexpected fire drills.

Jean did not have an easy time in other ways as well. She was born Jean Slutsky in Brooklyn, New York. Her father was a cab driver, and her mother was a manicurist. Although Jean was awarded a partial scholarship to Long Island University, the family's poor financial situation prevented her from attending. Instead, she enrolled in a business course at City College in New York. But again, she was forced to drop out when her father died. She was only nineteen at the time. So how did Jean manage to build a business empire without any formal education or financial support?

Here is Jean's success story. As a teenager and young adult, Jean tried many diets but did not persevere with any of them. In 1961, by this time a mother with two children, she was enrolled in the New York City Board of Health Obesity Clinic. Here she learned about healthy and appropriate food choices. Still she was not successful in losing weight, despite knowing all the right things to do and the right foods to eat.

As the narrative goes, one day Jean bumped into a woman at the supermarket who asked her when her baby was due. Jean was not pregnant but, at well over two hundred pounds, she knew she sure looked it. This embarrassing moment was the final straw and the impetus for Jean to change her eating habits. Jean knew she needed moral support if she was ever going to be able to maintain her resolve to adopt a healthier life style and lose weight. So, she solicited six friends, including Felice and Albert Lippert, to join her in her quest to lose weight and, more importantly, to keep it off.

The idea for the original weight loss program was very simple. The concept was to share the journey of lifestyle change and consequent weight loss with others in the same predicament. As Jean saw it, the principles for success were threefold. In addition to choosing a healthy balanced diet, each person in the group was responsible to keep a journal in which he or she recorded both healthy food choices and appropriate portion control. Remember Jean had learned about this at the Board of Health. Weekly meetings to report on progress and to encourage and support each other along the way were the second and third key components of the program.

Jean's diet concept proved successful. Within two months there were forty people in the group and soon word of mouth attracted hundreds more. In 1963, Jean and her friends and business partners, the Lipperts, incorporated Weight Watchers and developed a business plan that included rules for membership, recruitment of motivational leaders, meal plans, and cookbooks. By 1968, five million people were enrolled in Weight Watchers and in 1973, sixteen thousand people came to Madison Square Gardens in New York to celebrate its tenth anniversary. Even after Jean and the Lipperts sold the company, Jean remained its public face. She also maintained her goal weight for the remainder of her life.

Jean Nidetch was a woman who was able to turn a negative (her obesity) into a positive (her lucrative business) and in so doing, impact the wellbeing of millions of people worldwide. Jean intuited that sharing the experience of losing weight with others made the experience easier to cope with and therefore more likely to succeed. She recognized that sharing personal stories, listening to motivational speakers, and recording progress in a public forum could greatly enhance a person's ability to gain control over a goal or problem in his or her life. Today we know the therapeutic value of sharing experiences in a group setting, regardless of whether the life challenge is weight loss, cancer, schizophrenia, or bereavement, to name just a few.

Jean Nidetch is much more than a weight loss guru. She is a self-made woman with little formal education beyond high school. She is a pioneer in the promotion of the group support format as a powerful milieu for dealing with a challenging life situation. If Jean Nidetch were writing this sketch instead of me, she would advise you that if you ever need help for a problem in your life, don't be afraid or too proud to seek support from your family, your friends, or others in a similar situation. She would also likely tell you that it is "choice not chance" which determines the outcomes you achieve in your life.

RUTH PRAWER JHABVALA

RUTH PRAWER JHABVALA

MAY 7, 1927 - APRIL 3, 2013

DID YOU KNOW THAT SOME GIRLS KNOW AT A VERY YOUNG AGE WHAT THEY WANT TO BE WHEN THEY GROW UP?

Ruth Prawer Jhabvala was such a girl.

Ruth knew she was born to be a writer at age six. She was "flooded with (her) destiny" when she wrote her very first composition about a rabbit at Hebrew school in Cologne, Germany in 1933 (*The Guardian*, April 3, 2013). What she didn't know then was that she would go on to win the Booker prize for her fiction and two Oscar awards for her screenplays.

Ruth's life was a travel log of change and challenge. It is a life story that crosses four countries and three continents. She spent her childhood in Germany, her adolescent years in England, her child-rearing years in India, and her latter life in United States. No wonder her novels often speak of the displaced person's experience of alienation, acceptance, and foreign cultures.

For Ruth, the path to her destiny was long and winding. She was born in Germany where her maternal grandfather was the cantor in Cologne's largest synagogue. With her multi-generational roots in Cologne, Ruth's mother was reluctant to leave Germany in 1934 even after the Nazis arrested and later released both her and her Polish-born lawyer husband Marcus. In 1939, the family finally fled Germany and immigrated to England. It is said that Marcus Prawer lost his entire family in Poland during the Holocaust.

Ruth came to England in 1939 unable to speak any English. Within a year she was writing stories in English and, by 1951, she had a Master of Arts in English literature from Queen Mary College, University of London. That same year she married Cyrus Jhabvala, an architect from Delhi, India who she met while he was studying in England. Ruth moved to Delhi with him and was, for some time, enchanted by the sights, smells, and sounds of India.

For twenty or so years, she lived the life of a privileged Delhi housewife, raising three daughters and simultaneously launching her writing career. Her novels speak of her insights and interpretations of India. They are portrayals of the social mores and expectations of the India of her time, with its arranged marriages, exploitation of the poor, and corruption in business and government.

Over her career as a novelist, Ruth did not write of the Holocaust or about her life in Germany. She did, however, write of German Jewish characters who led dislocated but comfortable existences far from home. Ruth was torn between her European Jewish heritage and her British and Indian experiences. Uprootedness was the pattern of her life, and this theme of dislocation is prevalent in both her fiction and later, in her films.

Over time, Ruth became disillusioned with the poverty and squalor of India. This corresponded with her being approached by the American film producer and the American film director of Merchant Ivory Productions. Her screenplay *The Households* launched her career as a screenwriter for Hollywood movies. In 1975, to follow her dream and pursue a screenwriting career, Ruth moved to New York. So began the fourth phase of her life. That same year she also won the prestigious Booker Prize for her novel *Heat and Dust*. This literary award was followed by two Oscars at the Academy Awards for her adaptation to the movie screen of the novels *Room with a View* (1986) and *Howard's End* (1992), both by E. M. Forster. Ruth Prawer Jhabvala was both a famous writer of novels in India and an award-winning writer of movie scripts in America.

Ruth felt relatively comfortable living in America. She said that the delicatessens of New York provided her with the smoked meat, potato salads, and dill pickles of her childhood in Germany. New York also provided her with the camaraderie and language of the European Jewish people whose heritage was similar to her own. Although she initially had a commuter relationship with her husband, he eventually joined her permanently in New York.

Ruth Prawer Jhabvala was a girl who always knew that she wanted to be a writer. Over her lifetime, she let her unique gifts and talents guide her down paths and into environments she would never in a million years have dreamed possible as a first-grade student at Hebrew school in Cologne, Germany.

GERTRUDE ELION

GERTRUDE ELION

JANUARY 23, 1918 - FEBRUARY 21, 1999

DID YOU KNOW THAT A GIRL WHO BEGAN HER SCIENTIFIC CAREER MEASURING THE ACIDITY OF PICKLES FOR A GROCERY CHAIN COULD GO ON TO WIN A NOBEL PRIZE IN MEDICINE OR PHYSIOLOGY?

Gertrude (Trudy) Elion was that girl.

Mostly, this is a serious sketch because Trudy did very serious stuff over her lifetime. During her scientific career, she studied the difference between healthy and pathogenic (disease-causing) cells of the body and then engineered drugs to attack a particular pathogen. For example: Trudy and her colleague Dr. George Hitchings synthesized a drug which helped to cure leukemia in children. Pretty impressive for a girl who didn't have a Ph.D. or a medical degree!

While Trudy was totally devoted to her career, she also had a fun-spirited and playful side. She loved to travel and she especially loved listening to classical music. In 1998, during the Nobel Prize ceremony in Stockholm, Sweden, Trudy was seated on the podium waiting to receive her award when the orchestra started to play a Mozart aria. Rumour has it that Trudy tapped her foot and rocked her head in tune with the music. This was certainly a breach of expectation during the pomp and tradition of the Nobel Prize ceremony. But then again, Trudy was a breach of most expectations for a woman of her generation.

It is important to appreciate that the road to the Nobel was not a smooth or easy one for Trudy. As a young girl, she was a brilliant student. Her appetite for learning was encouraged by her Eastern European-born dentist father and her intelligent mother. By fifteen, Trudy had graduated from high school and was having difficulty deciding what to major in because she had loved all subjects in school equally. Around this time, her grandfather, who she was devoted to, died of cancer. Trudy decided to become a chemist and develop drugs to alleviate pain and suffering like that experienced by her Zaidy. When her fiancé died of an inflammation of the lining of the heart, her resolve to achieve scientific discovery and develop cures for disease was cemented.

Trudy achieved a Bachelor of Science from Hunter College and a Master of Science from New York University. But when she applied for fifteen fellowships, all of them were rejected because of gender bias. Academic institutions of the day did not take Trudy's interest in chemistry seriously simply because she was a woman, and science, especially chemistry, was a man's field. Even getting a job related to chemistry was a major challenge for Trudy.

Eventually, Trudy got a job as a food control supervisor testing the acidity of pickles, the colour of egg yolks in mayonnaise, and the quality of fruit in jams. This work was not very meaningful or inspiring for the scholarly and goal-oriented Trudy. But she might not have even got this job if World War II hadn't left a void in the job market with so many male candidates drafted into army duty. One day while she was working at this job, Trudy's father was given a sample of a painkiller to give his dental patients after surgery. He noticed that Burroughs Wellcome, a locally-based British drug company, had provided the sample. Trudy applied and secured a job at this pharmaceutical company. Her supervisor, Dr. George Hitchings, immediately recognized her intelligence and commitment.

Over the years, George and Trudy developed into a "dream team." Their forty years of collaboration revolutionized the pharmaceutical industry. Instead of trial and error, they used an approach called "rational drug design." Trudy and George examined the biochemistry of normal human cells and those of abnormal human cells. The abnormal cells included cancer cells, virus cells, and bacterial cells. They used the information they learned from examining the differences between how normal and abnormal cells reproduce to develop drugs that could kill or slow down the reproduction of the abnormal cells while, at the same time, leaving a person's healthy cells undamaged. This was both a "rational" and a novel approach.

So why did Trudy never earn a Ph.D.? Early on during her tenure at Burroughs Wellcome, she began to take courses towards her doctorate on a part-time basis while continuing work with Dr. Hitchings. But then, once again, she encountered unreasonable bias. The dean of the university told Trudy she had to enroll as a full-time student if she was serious about a doctoral degree. Trudy refused to quit her job. She knew her work with Dr. Hitchings was groundbreaking and potentially lifesaving and she was right.

She and Dr. Hitchings together with Sir Thomas Black discovered the principles of drug treatment effective against a whole host of diseases including cancer, malaria, herpes virus, and organ transplant rejection. The Nobel Prize committee, in making their decision, announced that any one of these discoveries would have been worthy of the Nobel. Later on, Trudy's team was even responsible for the pioneering treatment of Acquired Immune Deficiency (AIDS).

Despite never completing a formal Ph.D., Trudy received twenty-five honourary doctorates. When she received her first honourary degree from Washington University, Trudy, wanting to share the pride of her accomplishment, is quoted as saying, "I wish my mother were here" (cited in the Jewish Women's Archives from *Nobel Prize Women in Science: Their Lives, Struggles and Momentous Discoveries* by Sharon Bertsch McGrayne).

Gertrude Elion's first romantic love died when she was young. She never married nor had children of her own. However, she trained many future scientists and physicians. Through the Glaxo Wellcome program created in her honour, Trudy provided mentorship and funded scholarships for many women studying science. These generations of students became her "scientific" children and grandchildren.

Gertrude Elion was the first female inductee into the National Inventors Hall of Fame. She also received the National Medal of Science, the highest scientific award in the United States.

As quoted in the *Oncologist* in April, 1999, Gertrude Elion "showed us all, but perhaps particularly women, that difficulties can be overcome. She showed us all, but perhaps particularly children, the value of dreams." One of Gertrude Elion's famous quotes is "Don't be afraid of hard work. Nothing worthwhile comes easy. Don't let others discourage you or tell you that you can't do it" (Gertrude Elion, quoted in *Famous Scientists*). Gertrude Elion's advice to you and to other young people with hopes and aspirations would be simple: "Damn the torpedoes. Full speed ahead" (Admiral Farragut).

SONIA DELAUNAY

SONIA TERK DELAUNAY

NOVEMBER 14, 1845 - DECEMBER 5, 1979

DID YOU KNOW THAT CREATING A QUILT FOR HER NEWBORN SON COULD BE THE IMPETUS FOR A WOMAN TO START A NEW MOVEMENT IN ART?

Sonia Terk Delaunay was that woman.

Imagine you are both a new mother and an aspiring artist. You live in Paris but were born in Russia. You decide to make a quilt for your infant son's crib. To make this quilt you assemble multiple different fabrics of strong colours and bold geometric shapes. You recognize that in the design of this quilt, you have fused your childhood heritage in Russian folk art with concepts you adopted from the Parisian Cubist art movement. More importantly, you are very excited by the result and realize that this is the style of art you have been striving to achieve. Yes, Sonia Delaunay credited the inspiration for her paintings, costume, and textile design to the patchwork quilt she designed for her son Charles' crib.

Sonia Delaunay had a passion for exploring how primary and secondary colours would react when placed alongside each other in a painting. She found that the effect of marrying these seemingly conflicting colours was to create a phenomenon of "simultaneous contrast" where colours look different depending on those surrounding them. Sonia also found that the effect created movement and rhythm. She (and her husband Robert Delaunay) called this art "simultaneism" because of the energy it created. It was as if Sonia Delaunay's paintings and costume design literally made colours "dance." In fact, one of Sonia's earliest and most audacious paintings was *Le Bal Bullier*, named after a night club in the Latin Quarter of Paris she frequented with her husband. The painting portrays a row of dancers whose bodies become almost unrecognizable as they are broken into abstract segments of intense colour and movement on the canvas. The effect exemplified Sonia's focus on colour and movement over realistic form. A famous poet and art critic named Guillaume Apollinaire described Sonia's (and Robert's) art as Orphism because the bright colours of her work charmed viewers just like the mythical Greek musician and poet Orpheus had charmed objects with his music. The simultaneism practised by the Delaunays is considered a strand of the Orphism movement in art.

You will be interested to learn of Sonia's "colourful" childhood history. For a start, she was born Sarah Illinitchna Stern in the Ukraine, which was then part of the Russian empire. Her parents were hard-working peasants. Her mother had a brother named Henri Terk who was an affluent lawyer living in St. Petersburg, Russia. Little Sarah Stern was sent to live with the Terks in St. Petersburg where she soon adopted the name of Sonia Terk. Sonia lived a privileged and cultured life with the Terks, travelling in Europe and frequenting art galleries and museums. She learned to speak and read German, French, Russian, and English.

When her talent in art became apparent, the Terks sent Sonia to study at an exclusive art school in Germany. Recognizing that Paris, France was the "it" place for an emerging artist, the free-thinking and independent Sonia soon transferred to a school there. In an art gallery in Paris, she met key figures of the Paris avant-garde art scene including the Cubists Picasso and Braque. She also was introduced to the artist Robert Delaunay, with whom she established both a marriage and their version of the Simultaneous movement in Orphism art and design.

Sonia Delaunay had a career spanning some sixty years. She was a painter, a textile designer, a fashion and costume designer, and an entrepreneur. She collaborated with poets, choreographers, and manufacturers all in one lifetime. Here are some highlights of her career.

In 1911, Sonia designed her son's quilt, the model and impetus for her future endeavours. According to Sonia, there was no gap between her painting and her textile and decorative arts. For example, in 1913 she designed a dress for herself which she wore to a ball attended by the artists, musicians, and intellectuals of the day. Like she did with her son's quilt, to construct this dress, she interlocked oddly-shaped fabrics of abstract geometric patterns in varying sizes and dissonant colours. She even put colours like pink, orange, and scarlet together. Sonia literally dressed herself in her school of art and was the theory of Simultaneism in motion. This bold, dynamic style, which was an application of Orphism to clothing design, broke all traditions of the day and became a popular and sought-after style. Over her career, Sonia produced fashionable clothes which accentuated the sway and movement of the female body. Sonia considered these simultaneous style dresses as paintings to be worn.

While living in Spain during World War II, Sonia collaborated with Sergei Diaghilev, the famous choreographer and founder of the Ballet Russe, to design costumes for the ballet production of *Cleopatre*. Around 1921, Sonia, the designer, opened both a Simultaneous Studio where she created textiles and clothing as well as a fashion house called "Sonia" which catered to the avant-garde, famous actresses, and wealthy clients. In 1925, Sonia, the entrepreneur, began a collaboration with a department store in Amsterdam, Holland supplying them with fabric designs and home décor, a business relationship which lasted for several decades.

Sonia Delaunay was also a visionary who grasped the significance of the changes taking place in the world around her. She was able to capture the chaos and pace of modern life and give it form and substance. For example, in 1913, she collaborated with a poet named Blaise Cendrars to create a poem called *The Prose on the TransSiberian Railway* which describes a railway trip from Moscow to Paris. The text of the poem is interwoven with Sonia's patches of colour on the page. The goal was that the poet's text and Sonia's colour patches were to be read and viewed "simultaneously." Her abstract images and colour patches bend and sway and give the reader/viewer glimpses of the world outside the train. The effect was meant as an imitation of modern life with its electric lights, cars, and express trains. Remember that these inventions, which we take for granted, were all relatively new in 1913.

Sonia felt that this piece and other poem-paintings, like her textiles and dresses, extended simultaneous art beyond the confines of the artist's canvas into everyday life. She even painted her Citroen car in multi-coloured, abstract blocks. No wonder her Citroen became an icon of the jazz age period in which she lived!

Sonia Delaunay was the first living female artist to have a retrospective exhibit of her work at the Louvre Museum in Paris (1964).When President of France George Pompidou visited the then President of the United States Richard Nixon in Washington, Pompidou chose as a gift one of Sonia Delaunay's abstract circle paintings as representative of his country's finest achievements. In 1975, Sonia was awarded the Legion D'Honneur, France's highest accolade.

Sonia Delaunay was one of the pioneering forces in art and design of the twentieth century. One could say she thought that being bold with colour was a metaphor for being bold in life. At the onset of her career, Sonia struggled to find her niche in art. She came to realize that if you are searching for clarity in life and career, you should focus on what you know best. And that is what she did. Sonia took inspiration from her life experiences in Russia and Paris and from her son's baby blanket. Her bold colour choices and abstract patterns reflected her willingness to risk and experiment. Sonia Delaunay was a girl who was not afraid to pursue her passion, follow her instincts, and try something new.

LEA LENKE GOTTLIEB

LEA GOTTLIEB

SEPTEMBER 17, 1918 - NOVEMBER 17, 2012

DID YOU KNOW THAT A GIRL COULD HAVE BOTH A LOVE FOR THE SCIENCE OF CHEMISTRY AND A PASSION FOR THE ART OF DESIGN?

That girl was Lea Lenke Gottlieb.

To Lea, these two seemingly divergent interests share the same underlying process. To Lea, both chemistry and design involve creating something out of nothing by combining different "elements" with one other. Lea also said that, in planning for her future, she did not choose design over chemistry; rather, her life circumstances chose this for her.

Here is a short version of how Lea Gottlieb, or Lady Lea as she was known in the industry, became the world's most renowned bathing suit designer.

Lea Gottlieb was born Lea Lenke Roth in Sazoszent, Hungary. Her goal was to study chemistry in university but World War II interrupted her plan. Instead, she went to work as a bookkeeper/designer in a raincoat factory. Shortly after, she married Armin Gottlieb, a member of the family that owned the factory. During the Nazi occupation of Hungary, Armin was shipped to a labour camp and Lea had to use all of her wits to secure hiding places for herself and her two daughters. In order to hide her obviously Jewish-looking face at German checkpoints, Lea reported that she would tuck her head into a bouquet of flowers so she could pass as one of the peasant girls on the street. Lea once said that she often used flower motifs in her swimsuit designs because she credited flowers with saving her life.

In 1949, after the war, Lea and her family made aliyah to the newly born State of Israel where they opened a raincoat factory. Lea quickly realized the folly in this decision. It was sensible to produce raincoats in cold, rainy Hungary, but it was foolish to do so in sunny, seaside Israel. The resilient Lea changed her product and began to design and manufacture swimsuits, a garment much better suited to the Israeli climate and lifestyle. It has been said that Lea had to sell her wedding ring to buy fabric, as well as borrow a sewing machine from friends, in order to start this business.

Lea's design vision was novel to the marketplace. Not only did she inject glamour into swimwear. but she also introduced the concept that bathing suits should be able to travel from the patio and pool to restaurants and parties. To accomplish this, Lea designed and produced caftans, skirts, tunics, and pants to coordinate with her swimsuits. She even designed the fabrics herself and had them woven in Italy to her exacting specifications. That is why her line of bathing suits is called Gottex: "Got" from Gottlieb and "tex" from the textiles she designed. Much of Lea's textiles had an Israeli influence including the burnt yellow of the desert sand, the azure blue of the Mediterranean Sea, and the rich green of the fertile Galilee area of Israel. Her most personally treasured collection was the Jerusalem of Gold (1992) series. It refers to the gold jewel, most likely a necklace, which Rabbi Akiva gave to his wife Rachel as a sign of love. The gorgeous ornaments embedded in the bathing suits and clothes of this collection were drawn from Jewish symbolism and include the Star of David, a menorah, and a breast plate with twelve gems in twelve squares representing the twelve tribes of Israel. Judaism was very important to Lea. That is why, after her death, about thirty items from the Jerusalem of Gold collection were found in her bedroom drawer, beside her siddur (prayer book).

The sources of Lea's inspiration were not limited to Jewish themes. Famous artists like Van Gogh and Gauguin and ideas from ancient Egyptian mythology also sparked her imagination and guided her designs. Gottex bathing suits became the go-to bathing suits for movie stars like Elizabeth Taylor, and royalty like Princess Caroline of Monaco. Princess Diana of England even had a kangaroo-design swimsuit custom-made by Lady Lea when she went to visit Australia!

Gottex became Israel's leading fashion exporter, selling to more than eighty countries worldwide. At the Yad Vashem, "My Homeland-Holocaust Survivors in Israel" tribute (2008), the largest space in the exhibition was allocated to Lea Gottlieb for her role in Israel's economic and cultural development.

To Lea Gottlieb, water was a phenomenon which necessitated attire appropriate to the climate and environment. In the final analysis, it did not matter whether Lea was designing a raincoat or a bathing suit. What did make the difference to Lea's success was her fierce determination, her willingness to learn from her mistakes, and her capacity to adapt to obstacles and changing life circumstances. If Lea were writing this sketch instead of me, she would tell you to capitalize on your acquired skills and natural talents (regardless of whether these are cooking, chemistry, or calculus). She would tell you to be to be resilient and to stay focused on your end goal. Then you too will be able to make it work!

HEDY LAMARR

HEDY LAMARR

NOVEMBER 9, 1914 - JANUARY 19, 2000

DID YOU KNOW THAT A GIRL COULD GROW UP TO BE
BOTH A FAMOUS MOVIE STAR AND A PIONEER INVENTOR
IN THE FIELD OF WIRELESS TECHNOLOGY?

Hedwig Eva Maria Kiesler, known in the film industry as Hedy Lamarr, was that girl.

The story of Hedy Lamarr is unbelievable and the opposite of what people think. Hedy was indeed a study in contradiction — a beautiful, glamorous actress by day and a self-taught, brilliant inventor by night. Her acting gave her fame and glory but her discoveries helped change the world. Just what is the story behind this enigmatic woman and her double life?

Hedy was an only child born to a cultured and affluent family in Vienna, Austria. As a youngster, her mathematical skills and technical intuition were recognized by her father. You see, Hedy demanded that her father provide explanations for how anything and everything mechanical and technical, from street cars to printing presses, functioned. As a teenager, Hedy attended finishing school in Switzerland and later studied acting. By the time she was seventeen, Hedy had starred in her first movie. A short while later, while performing in a stage play, an admirer named Friedrich (Fritz) Mandl, enamoured with her stage presence, sent roses to her dressing room as an excuse to meet her. Hedy was talented and aspiring; Fritz was distinguished and prosperous. They were married soon after. While her father encouraged Hedy to think independently, make her own decisions, and control her own destiny, he was against this marriage. Hedy too soon realized she had made a poor decision in her choice of husband. Hedy was goal-oriented and determined while Fritz was domineering and controlling. Fritz not only prevented Hedy from pursuing her acting career but he also made her feel like a prisoner in her castle-like home of twenty-five rooms. Fritz treated Hedy like a rare collectable object which had to be carefully guarded. This role did not suit Hedy. As she remarked, "Any girl can be glamorous. All you have to do is stand still and look stupid" (quoted in *The Guardian*, July 29, 1999).

Nonetheless, history suggests that this poor marriage decision ultimately had good future consequences for Hedy. You see, Fritz was a military arms manufacturer. Because of her mathematical prowess and presence as a hostess, Fritz often included Hedy in meetings and dinner parties with scientists and politicians who were involved in the development and production of military technology. Torpedoes and radio technologies were frequent topics of discussion. As she was an extremely good listener and a quick learner, these meetings sparked Hedy's interest and natural talent in the field of applied science.

One night when Fritz was away, Hedy escaped from her stifling environment. Meanwhile, Louis B. Mayer, the famous Hollywood movie producer and co-founder of Metro Goldwyn Mayer, was in Europe scouting for talent. A film agent in London, England took Hedy to a hotel to meet Mr. Mayer. He brought Hedy to Hollywood, California and promoted her as the world's most beautiful woman. It has been reported that when Hedy debuted in the movie *Algiers* (1938), the audience gasped when she first appeared on the screen. Her presence literally took their breath away!

Despite her successes, Hedy became disenchanted with the movie business. She felt that her roles limited her scope and didn't showcase her talent. Bored with the lack of challenge, she began to pursue her hobby of inventing more seriously.

During this time, Hedy was friends with the famous aviation tycoon Howard Hughes. His goal was to make the world's fastest airplane. Hedy presented Hughes with ideas on how to make the wings of a plane less square and therefore more efficient. To deduce her ideas, the creative Hedy had studied the aerodynamics of birds and the shapes of fish. Howard Hughes, recognizing her genius, offered to support any scientific endeavour Hedy chose to pursue.

Meanwhile, World War II was raging in Europe. Hedy read that two ocean liners carrying Jewish children to safety were torpedoed by the Germans. Hedy, always conscious of her Jewish heritage, wanted to make a contribution to the war effort. So, when the National Inventors Council of the United States asked Americans to contribute ideas for defence devices, Hedy responded.

Here is the background to her invention. Hedy had learned that radio was an unreliable way to control American torpedoes because the Nazis, or other enemies, could easily jam the signals, causing the torpedoes to veer off course and miss the enemy target. Remember that while still married to Fritz, Hedy had been an astute listener during the discussions of military arms technology. Hedy was able to apply the knowledge she had gained from this exposure in Vienna to figure out how to overcome this problem of how to guide American torpedoes. Together with George Anheil and financing from Hughes, Hedy designed a secret communication system which involved sending signals over different and changing frequencies. She called this process "frequency hopping."

Hedy's purpose in designing this communication system was to combat the Nazis in World War II. Her invention formed an unbreakable code which prevented information from being intercepted by the Nazis and other enemies.

Unfortunately, Hedy's genius was not appreciated in her day. She was told that she could make a greater contribution to the war effort "as a pinup rather than an inventor: entertaining the troops, pushing war bonds and…selling kisses" (*The Guardian*, March 8, 2018). Metro Goldwyn Mayer also did not promote Hedy's scientific work because it did not fit with their marketing strategy. Hedy was supposed to be beautiful, not brilliant. As a result, the full significance of Hedy's discovery was not realized until decades after she invented it. The technology, now called "broad spectrum technology," helped to create the technical resource support that makes our present-day WiFi, Bluetooth, and GPS operations possible. Yes, we can also thank Hedy Lamarr for our cell phones and fax machines!

For her pioneering work in the field of wireless communication, in 1997, Hedy Lamarr and George Anheil received the BULBIE Gnass Spirit of Achievement Award, an award given to individuals whose contribution to science has significantly benefitted society. This award is often called the Oscar of invention. In the end, Hedy Lamarr considered the "Oscar" for her scientific invention to be the best award of her lifetime. For Hedy, it was her contribution as an inventor, not her applause as an actor, from which she derived the greatest meaning in life.

Hedy Lamarr was a woman of formidable intelligence and technological vision at a time when society was unwilling to recognize or appreciate that these could co-exist in a beautiful woman. Hedy Lamarr was a true "star" who has finally been credited with leaving an indelible mark in the world of wireless communications. In recognition of her achievement, Inventors' Day in Austria, Germany, and Switzerland is celebrated on November 9, her birthday.

NADINE GORDIMER

NADINE GORDIMER

NOVEMBER 20, 1923 - JULY 13, 2014

DID YOU KNOW THAT A WOMAN WHOSE NOVELS WERE BANNED IN SOUTH AFRICA COULD WIN A NOBEL PRIZE FOR HER NOVELS ABOUT SOUTH AFRICA?

That woman was Nadine Gordimer.

Here is a review of some background information about South Africa so you can better appreciate this sketch. From 1948 to the early 1990s, South Africa had a political ideology and system of government called apartheid. Apartheid is the Afrikaans word for apartness or separateness. Basically, apartheid made it legal to segregate and discriminate against Black, Mixed Race, and Asian (Indian and Pakistani) South Africans. On the basis of race, the state determined where these people lived, how they were educated, who they could marry, where they could shop, and even which park benches they could sit on.

During apartheid years, there was much resistance to these government policies. Sometimes, this was achieved through nonviolent demonstrations and protests. Other times, objection was more militant and involved political actions including strikes against the government and even armed resistance. One protestor, Nadine Gordimer, used the power of pen and paper to raise her voice against apartheid. It was through the vehicle of her novels that Nadine Gordimer's protest against the horrors of South Africa's injustices was heard all over the world.

Nadine was born in a gold mining town just south of Johannesburg, South Africa. Her father was an uneducated refugee from Eastern Europe who left school at age eleven to learn the trade of watch making and repair. Her mother, Hannah (Nan) Myers, came to South Africa at age six from England. It was from her mother that Nadine first learned of activism and concern for the plight of Black South Africans. Nan's influence on Nadine was also felt in another way. She removed Nadine from school for a presumed heart ailment at age eleven and Nadine was then home-schooled until age sixteen. This left Nadine isolated from social contact with her peers. At the same time, it fostered her reading and writing abilities and resulted in her publishing her first stories in newspapers and magazines as a teenager.

During her year at University of the Witwatersrand, Nadine was captivated by the bohemian, free-thinking lifestyle she was exposed to. Her introduction to Sophiatown, one of Johannesburg's black townships, and to black writers and artists, was a major catalyst for both her activism and her future literary works.

Nadine Gordimer's literary works provide a social and political history of the South Africa of her day. Her early novels chronicle the lives of ordinary people, both black and white, in a segregated society. Her themes revolve around love and the injustices of racial discrimination and division. Her characters inhabit both black shanty towns and elite white neighbourhoods.

Because of the contempt for the apartheid system of government expressed in her novels, three of Gordimer's novels were banned in South Africa during the apartheid era. Censorship of *A World of Strangers* lasted twelve years. Yet during this time, Gordimer's novels were widely read and praised by the international literary community. Her novels awoke the conscience of the world to the cruelty and injustice of the apartheid regime. Her later novels also mirror stages and changes in South African history. In these later novels, Nadine predicts the end of the apartheid regime and subsequently chronicles the issues which would surface with its collapse and the country's national rebirth.

Gordimer's novels were indeed prophetic. In 1990, Nelson Mandela, a lawyer, political activist, and close friend of Nadine's who later became the first black president, was released from prison, apartheid laws were repealed, the African National Party regained legal standing, and democratic elections were held in 1994.

Like Mandela, Nadine Gordimer also was a political activist. She joined the African National Congress (ANC) when it was listed as illegal, spoke out against political repression, and even hid ANC leaders in her home so they could avoid being arrested. She testified in defence of those accused of treason against the state and helped edit Nelson Mandela's famous speech "I am prepared to die" (for a free society and democracy) delivered from the defendant's dock at his trial. When Nelson Mandela was finally released from prison, his friend Nadine Gordimer was one of the first people he asked to see.

In the post-apartheid 1990s, Nadine's activism was directed to the fight against HIV/AIDS. She organized twenty famous writers to contribute a short story for *Telling Tales*, a book used to lobby funding for HIV/AIDS prevention and treatment.

In 1974, Nadine Gordimer won the Booker prize (now Man Booker) for her novel *The Conservationist*. In October 1991, she was awarded the Nobel Prize for Literature for her extensive body of work. In the words of Alfred Nobel, "through her magnificent epic writing," Nadine Gordimer "has been of very great benefit to humanity" (*New York Times*, October 4, 1991). People praised Gordimer for both her writing and for her political activism, but she considered herself first and foremost a writer, not an activist. In an interview, Nadine was once asked, "Can literature make a difference?" Gordimer replied that it has always done so. She replied, "literature, poetry, novels, stories — these are an exploration of life" (*New Statesman America*, June 4, 2010).

Through her novels, Nadine Gordimer explored life in apartheid South Africa. Her explorations opened the eyes of the world to the horrors of apartheid. Her message of freedom and justice for all South Africans was instrumental in effecting change in her country. Nadine Gordimer would say that freedom and justice should exist in every country in the world!

EDITH HEAD

EDITH HEAD

OCTOBER 28, 1897 - OCTOBER 24, 1981

DID YOU KNOW THAT THE WOMAN WHO DESIGNED THE VERY FIRST UNITED STATES COAST GUARD UNIFORMS FOR WOMEN WAS ALSO THE "DOCTOR" OF DRESS DESIGN TO FAMOUS HOLLYWOOD ACTRESSES OF HER DAY?

Edith Head was that woman.

Imagine a woman with a short, black bob haircut and bangs who wears thick, round glasses. Does this remind you of anyone? Hint. It is possible that this trademark "look" was the inspiration for Edna Mode, the animated character in *The Incredibles* movies. Edna Mode made clothes for a family of super heroes. Edith Head made costumes for superstars like Elizabeth Taylor, Marilyn Munroe, and Audrey Hepburn. Edith herself became a superhero and superstar costume designer with eight Oscars and thirty-five Oscar nominations. It was Edith who lobbied The Motion Picture Arts and Sciences to include costume design as a category for Oscar at the Academy Awards. She even had a dedicated Google Doodle on what would have been her 116th birthday!

Edith Head is the story of a self-made woman who rose through the ranks at Paramount Studios in Hollywood, California to become the first female chief designer of a movie studio. As you read

Edith's story, you will realize that she achieved this through both self-promotion and just plain chutzpah.

Edith Head was born Edith Claire Posener. Her parents divorced when she was young and her mother remarried a mining engineer whose job necessitated that the family move many times while Edith was growing up. Because the family didn't establish roots in any one place, it was hard for Edith to develop friendships. No sooner did she find a playmate than the family would relocate once again.

As a young girl, Edith liked to sew and make clothes. While she was living in Nevada, Edith reported that she had no playmates, so she relied on vermin of the desert, like toads, to be the models for her clothing designs. One could say this was the beginning of her career in costume design. Later in life, the resourceful Edith is quoted as saying something like this: if you can dress a horned toad, you can dress anything.

For a girl of her generation, Edith was very well-educated. She achieved a Bachelor of Arts (with Honours) in French from University of Southern California and a Master of Arts in Romance Languages from Stanford University. In 1924, she was teaching French at Hollywood School for Girls during the day and studying art at Chouinard Art Institute in the evenings.

One day, Edith saw a classified advertisement in the *Los Angeles Times*. The Famous Players-Lasky movie studio (which became Paramount Studios) needed a sketch artist to create costumes for films. Edith wanted this job and she wanted it badly! Trouble was, she was not fully qualified for it. This did not deter the ambitious Edith. She presented herself for interview with a fabricated portfolio of diverse talent much of which she had borrowed from her colleagues at Chouinard. While one cannot in any way condone this kind of indiscretion, one can admire Edith's strong determination to succeed. She confessed her falsehood to her boss who was so impressed with her determination and ability to promote herself that he hired and trained her anyway. With tutoring and practise, Edith was able to enhance her natural talent for design and became the go-to dress designer for most of the famous movie stars of her time.

In Edith's day, men ran the movie studios and men dominated as costume designers. Actresses didn't have much of a voice in their costume selection. Instead, they were expected to wear what was suggested to them by the male designers. Edith revolutionized this scenario. She spent time conversing with the actresses and developing a barometer for what they liked to wear and what they felt good in. While this may seem an obvious method for costume design today, it was a major break with the prevailing protocol. One could say Edith approached design like a "doctor" with individualized attention to each actress's unique taste, body shape, and personality. Her goal was to accentuate the positive and minimize the flaws. As she famously remarked, "What a costume designer does is a cross between magic and camouflage" (*Telegraph*, August 14, 2104).

At the studio, Edith dressed in dull grey so she could disappear into the background while the actresses could shine. Outside of the studio, Edith did not fade into the background. She became a fashion authority for women, giving advice on dress and demeanour, in magazines, on television, and in two bestselling books entitled *The Dress Doctor* and *Dressing for Success*. She suggested to women that they think of themselves as a product and that in order to achieve success they needed to sell the product. Her advice was to immediately start thinking of ways to improve the product. Likely, she would have agreed this goes for anything, from power dressing to PowerPoint presentations. Remember to think of Edith when you are disappointed or discouraged with the outcome of a life event or decision. Edith likely would say try "packaging" yourself differently.

In 1938, Edith Head broke the glass ceiling when she was named the first female designer of a major motion picture studio. Had she been born in a different time, perhaps she would have even run the studio.

HENRIETTA SZOLD

HENRIETTA SZOLD

DECEMBER 21, 1860 - FEBRUARY 13, 1945

DID YOU KNOW THAT FOR MANY YEARS MOTHER'S DAY IN ISRAEL
WAS CELEBRATED TO HONOUR THE YAHRZEIT (ANNIVERSARY OF
DEATH) OF AN AMERICAN WOMAN FROM BALTIMORE, MARYLAND?

Henrietta Szold was that woman.

This biographical sketch has its origin in a biblical story. Long ago, a Jewish girl named Hadassah won a beauty pageant and was chosen to marry Ahasuerus, the King of Persia. Hadassah became the biblical Queen Esther who saved the Jewish people from annihilation by the wicked tyrant Haman. Every year since then, the salvation of the Jewish people is celebrated as the holiday of Purim. One of the responsibilities of Jews on Purim, both in biblical times and today, is the virtue of giving to others. This custom is derived from the name Hadassah. The name Hadassah has its roots in the word "hadas," the Hebrew name for the myrtle tree. In the Talmud, righteous people are called myrtles because, like the myrtle tree, they are sweet and good. Based on Talmudic interpretation, the name Hadassah symbolizes righteousness, compassion, and caring. With this as background, I invite you to read about Henrietta Szold and "Hadassah," the worldwide Zionist organization dedicated to the virtue of helping the Jewish people by doing practical work in Israel.

Henrietta Szold was such an incredibly remarkable woman that it is difficult to capture her major influence on the Jewish world of her time in just one or two descriptors.

Henrietta was a teacher, a social worker, an author, a translator, an editor, an organizational genius, an early feminist, and a true visionary. But perhaps the most all-encompassing way to describe her is best expressed in the singular noun "Zionist." Her vision and achievement were to create and support a Jewish state in Palestine. For this reason, Henrietta Szold is considered "Mother of the Yeshuv," Mother of the Jewish people in Palestine.

It is also difficult to capture Henrietta's major contributions to Zionism and the Jewish people of Palestine in just one or two words. But perhaps this too is best encapsulated in a singular noun, "Hadassah." Henrietta Szold was the founder and the first president of Hadassah, the American Zionist organization dedicated to improving health and living conditions in pre and post-statehood Israel. By the way, Hadassah is still very active today and I would hazard a guess that if you ask around, you will learn that someone you know is a member of the organization.

Henrietta was the daughter of a rabbi and the eldest of her parents Benjamin and Sophie's eight daughters. Recognizing her piercing intellect, her father taught her the Talmud, Bible, and Jewish history. She also mastered Latin as well as the German, French, and Hebrew languages. Although she graduated from high school as valedictorian, Henrietta did not consider leaving home to attend university. The emerging colleges for girls were outside of Baltimore and, in those days, a Jewish girl did not leave her parents' home, except to marry. So, Henrietta became a teacher in a private school. While working as a teacher, she also wrote articles and became a regular contributor to the *Jewish Messenger*, a journal which was published in New York. Under the pen name Sulamith, she wrote of her observations and her critiques of American Jewish culture. While being a woman initially presented a credibility concern, through these articles, Henrietta's voice was beginning to be heard.

In the late 1800s, Russian and other Eastern European Jewish immigrants began to arrive in Baltimore, fleeing the pogroms and persecution in their countries of origin. While maintaining her day job, Henrietta was able to organize and serve as principal of a night school whose goals were to train these immigrants in the English language, help acculturate them to their new country, and teach them practical vocational skills. You could say that Henrietta Szold developed the first English as a Second Language program and vocational support system for Jewish immigrants in Baltimore. Eventually, the public school system in Baltimore even incorporated her program into its curriculum. As an aside, in Toronto, Canada, there is still a program which supports immigrants in resettlement and vocational skills training. This used to be called Jewish Vocational Services but was renamed as the program expanded to support people of all races, religions, and ethnicities.

In 1893, Henrietta moved to Philadelphia to become the sole woman at the Jewish Publication Society, a position she held for over twenty years. Her official title was secretary but, in reality, she was their first editor overseeing the publication of eighty-seven books during her tenure. Her objective was to bring works of Jewish culture to the Jews of America. For example, she produced and edited the first American Jewish Yearbook and collaborated to compile a Jewish encyclopedia. In 1893, Henrietta also became a member of the Zionist Association of Baltimore and, in 1896, she published a lecture outlining her Zionist belief in the need to create and support a Jewish homeland in Palestine to ensure that Jews did not face extinction. In 1898, Henrietta was elected the only female member of the Federation of American Zionists Executive Committee.

To enrich her understanding of Jewish texts and enhance her ability to translate and edit her father's papers, in 1902, Henrietta moved to New York where she attended classes at the Jewish Theological Seminary, an all-male institution. She was the seminary's first female student and was admitted as a special student under special dispensation. This included the proviso that she not seek ordination as a rabbi. You can read between the lines to appreciate the feelings of frustration and constraint a woman of Henrietta's brilliance and competence must have experienced. Today we credit her with being a pioneering feminist who accomplished many "firsts" for women, especially Jewish women, of her day.

As you have read above, Henrietta played a seminal role in creating a meaningful Jewish culture in America through her efforts as a teacher, essayist, editor, feminist, and early theoretical Zionist. But it was during her first trip to Palestine in 1909, at age forty-nine, that she realized her true mission in life. On this trip, Henrietta was horrified by the poverty and disease of the Jews, Muslims, and

Christians of Palestine. She recognized the urgent need to bring health care, education, and social welfare to the people of Palestine. She realized it was time to stop talking about building a Jewish homeland in Palestine and time to start doing something productive to ensure its creation. Moreover, Henrietta was convinced that American Jewish women were the ones who could help make this happen.

Upon her return from Palestine, Henrietta addressed a group of women at a synagogue in New York. She told the women it was time to "stop drinking tea" and theorizing about Zionism. It was time to do something "real and practical" like sending doctors and nurses to Palestine. It was Purim, February 24, 1912 and the organization was given the name Hadassah, the Talmudic word for compassion and caring. Like Hadassah, the heroine of the Purim story, the Hadassah Zionist organization would save the Jewish people from annihilation by establishing a Jewish homeland in Palestine. Henrietta Szold became Hadassah's first president and, over time, Hadassah became one of the largest Zionist organization in North America and the largest Jewish women's organization in the world.

Under Henrietta Szold's organizational genius, in 1913, the medical efforts of Hadassah in Palestine saw five thousand patients in the first year. By 1918, Hadassah was able to outfit a small hospital with forty-five doctors and nurses as well as four hundred tons of supplies and medical equipment that had never before been seen in Palestine. The efforts of Hadassah, under Henrietta's leadership, had revolutionized medical care in Palestine. By 1920, when Henrietta made aliyah to Palestine and took over full executive responsibility of the medical unit, she had transformed it into an organization that emphasized the health needs of women and children, including food programs and milk clinics and a nursing school. The value and influence of Hadassah was now firmly established throughout Palestine. Years later, in 1934, Henrietta spoke at the laying of the cornerstone ceremony of the new Hadassah Hospital on Mt Scopus in Jerusalem. If you go to Israel today you should visit Hadassah Hospital and the Henrietta Szold School of Nursing.

Henrietta also was appointed to influential roles in the Palestine Jewish community. In this capacity, she helped to create the infrastructure of the future state of Israel. Her portfolio included not only health but also the system of social welfare and education that defined Israel when it was founded in 1948.

And one more thing: with the rise of Hitler and the Nazi threat, Henrietta helped spearhead the Youth Aliyah program. Between 1933 and 1945, Youth Aliyah brought thirty thousand child victims of Nazi persecution to Palestine. Try to conceive of the organizational challenges she and her colleagues must have faced. To relocate these children, Henrietta and her colleagues had to arrange for the children's transportation, secure their visas, and then establish emotional support and education systems for the homeless and motherless orphans once they got to Palestine. No wonder she was considered "Mother of the Yishuv" and that Mother's Day in Israel was held on the anniversary of her death!

Henrietta Szold is the last entry in this manuscript for good reason. She was a teacher without a teaching certificate, a social worker without social work credentials, a writer and editor with no formal journalism training, a Judaic scholar without rabbical ordination, a hospital administrator without a business degree, and a politician who helped to create the infrastructure of modern-day Israel. Henrietta was also an early feminist whose greatest legacy, Hadassah, is a model of what Jewish women can do to transform and define Jewish communal life. Henrietta Szold not only proved the power of the activism of women but she also taught us that women can, indeed, change the world. To quote Henrietta Szold's challenge, as reported in *Hadassah Magazine* on October 5, 2016: "Dare to dream…and when you dream, dream big."

SOURCES

Researching the biographies of the eighteen trailblazing Jewish women profiled in *Jewish Girls Who Dreamed Big and Changed* the World was enlightening and fun. If you want to learn more about these women, here is a list of some of the sources I consulted to carry out my research.

www.barbiemedia.com

www.bbc.com/news/technology

www.biography.com

www.britannica.com/people

www.famousscientists.org/

www.forbes.com.2018/this-woman-change-the-way...

www.theguardian.com/tone(name of deceased)

www.haaretz.com/(person's name)

www.huffingtonpost.com/(name of deceased)

www.thejc.com/news/(person's name) (jc is Jewish Chronicle)

www.jwa.org/encyclopedia (jwa is Jewish Women's Archive)

www.jewishvirtuallibrary.org/(person's name)

www.nytimes.com/(person's name)

www.nobelprize.org(recipient's name)

www.tabletmagazine.com/(person's name)

www.thoughtco.com/(person's name)

www.timesofisrael.com/(person's name)

www.wikipedia.org

www.yadvashem.org/(person's name)

Here is a list of the specific articles from journals, newspapers, and magazines quoted in *Jewish Girls Who Dreamed Big and Changed the World*. These are cited in the order they appear in the text of the book.

InStyle Magazine, March 2019.

Atkinson, Nathalie. "Barbie at 60: Why Does the Iconic Doll Feel Like All Work and No Play?" *The Globe and Mail*. March 3, 2019. Retrieved from https://www.theglobeandmail.comlife/style/article-barbie-at-60-all-work-and-no-play/

Berry, Jennifer. "Tessa Virtue Is Now a Barbie Doll-and She Is Stoked." *The Kit*. March 7, 2019. Retrieved from https://the kit.ca/life/celebrity-life/tessa-virtue-barbie-doll

McFadden, Robert. "Evelyn Berezin, 93, dies; built the First True Word Processor." *The New York Times*. December 10, 2018. Retrieved from https://www.nytimes.com/2018/12/10/obituaries/evelyn-berezin-dead.html

Nemy, Enid. "Judith Leiber, 97, Dies; Turned Handbags into Objets d'Art." *The New York Times*. April 30, 2018. Retrieved from https://www.nytimes/.../judith-leiber-97-dies-turned-handbags-into-objets-dart-html

Anderson, Jon. "Advice columnist Ann Landers dead at 83." *Chicago Tribune*. June 22, 2002. Retrieved from https://www.chicagotribune.com/news/chi-020622/landers-story-htbl

Currie, Bennie. "Renowned advice columnist Ann Landers dies." *The Seattle Times*. June 23, 2002. Retrieved from community.seattletimes.nwresource.com/archive?date=20020623&slug=ann230

D'Ormesson, Jean. "Simone Veil is interred in the Parthenon." *The Atlantic*. Retrieved from https://www.the atlantic.com/international/archive/2018/10/07/simone-veil.../564269

Fox, Sylvan. "Tragedy of the Jewish People." *The New York Times*. May 13, 1970. Retrieved from https://www.nytimes/.../nelly-sachs-poet-dead-at-78-won-nobel-prize-for literature

Watts, Janet. "Ruth Prawer Jhabvala Obituary." *The Guardian*. April 3, 2013. Retrieved from https://www.the guardian.com/books/2013/april/03-ruth-prawer-jhabvala

Elion, Gertrude. "I wish my mother were here." *Jewish Women's Archives*. Retrieved from https://www.jwa.org/women of valor/Elion

Ingram, Robert et al. "Tributes to Gertrude Elion." *The Oncologist*. April, 1999.

Elion, Gertrude. "Don't be afraid of hard work." *Famous Scientists*. Retrieved from Famousscientists. org/gertrude-b-elion

Lamarr, Hedy. "Any girl can be glamorous. All you have to do is stand still and look stupid." *The Guardian*. July 29, 1999. Retrieved from https://www.the guardian.com/…hedy-lamarr-1940 s-bombshell-helped-invent-wifi

Lamarr, Hedy. "…to the war effort as a pinup rather than as an inventor." The Guardian. March 18, 2018. https://www.the guardian.com/…2018/mar/…hedy-lamarr-1940s-bombshell-

Craig, Whitney. "Nadine Gordimer Is Winner of Nobel Prize in Literature." *The New York Times*. October 4, 1991. Retrieved from https://www.nytimes.com/nadine-gordimer-is-winner...html

Shackle, Samira. "Interview with Nadine Gordimer." *New Statesman*. June 4, 2010. Retrieved from https://www.newstatesman.com/Africa/2010/06-interview-life-vote

Sowray, Bibby. "Why Costume Designer Edith Head Should Not Be Forgotten." *Telegraph*. August 14, 2014. Retrieved from https://www.fashion.telegraph.co.uk/…why-costume-designer-edit h-head-should-

Hershkin, Ellen. "Dreaming Big." *Hadassah Magazine*. October, 2016. Retrieved from www.hadassahmagazine.org/2016/10/05.

Here is a list of some of the books that helped me write *Jewish Girls Who Dreamed Big and Changed the World*.

Felder, Deborah and Diana Rosen. *Fifty Jewish Women Who Changed the World*. New York: Kensington Publishing, 2003.

Ignotofsky, Rachel. *Women in Science: 50 Fearless Pioneers-Who Changed the World*. Berkeley: Ten Speed Press, Crown Publishing, 2016.

Lawrence, Sandra. *Anthology of Amazing Women: Trailblazers Who Dared to Be Different*. New York: Little Bee Books, Bonnier Publishing, 2018.

Segal, Sheila. *Women of Valor: Stories of Great Jewish Women Who Helped Shape the Twentieth Century*. New York: Behrman House Inc., 1996.

Shen, Ann. *Bad Girls Throughout History: 100 Remarkable Women Who Changed the World*. San Francisco, California: Chronicle Books, 2016.

Skeers, Linda. *Women Who Dared: 52 Stories of Fearless Daredevils, Adventurers, Rebels*. Naperville, Illinois: Sourcebooks, Inc., 2017

Swaby, Rachel. *Trailblazers: 33 Women in Science Who Changed the World*. New York: Delacorte Press, 2016.

CPSIA information can be obtained
at www.ICGtesting.com
Printed in the USA
BVHW091331180819
555967BV00027B/166/P